# WITHDRAWN

## DATE DUE

| | | | |
|---|---|---|---|
| DEC 1 2 | | | |
| JAN 0 9 2014 | | | |

# Praise for *Making Telework Work*

"*Making Telework Work* is a timely and invaluable book for any leader whose supervisory responsibilities extend not only domestically but globally. Offstein and Morwick are masters on this topic, having spent their careers helping others and presenting a seemingly daunting concept into an easy to learn, step-by-step process . . . this timely and important book is essential. This is not for the faint-hearted. It's relevant and powerful and a *must-read* for the manager who wants to succeed in today's competitive global economy NOW."
—Ralph Jordan, President / CEO of Trident Health Resources, Inc.

"With higher gas prices, deteriorating infrastructures, and the demands for more flexible schedules from younger workers, telework is not just a 'good idea,' it has become an imperative. The authors lay out, in an easy-to-read format, how to move from idea to implementation of something I predict within the next generation will be the norm."
—Dr. Miles K. Davis, Associate Professor of Management and Director of the Institute for Entrepreneurship in the Harry F. Byrd Jr. School of Business at Shenandoah University

"It goes without saying that our world has changed. . . . The way we do work has changed and the way we need to think about work has changed. . . . This is truly the book on leadership strategies to make work environments more effective and efficient and is a welcome book to drive leaders to create these interactive environments."
—Jonathan C. Gibralter, President, Frostburg State University

"Finally, a real how-to-manage telework set of guidelines has been published. . . . The authors dissect the management problems for teleworking, then provide solutions that have solid application in managing any team, distributed or not. Read this book . . . before committing to a telework strategy in your organization."
—Thomas W. Mastaglio, Ph.D., President and CEO MYMIC LLC

"The Internet provides us worldwide access to information. Today's leadership must recognize that the beneficial use of that information will involve an ever increasing need for collaborations and new relationships with subject matter experts to transform into knowledge leading to innovations."
—Thomas Lamb, Chief, Innovation and Technology, New York City Transit, Capital Program Management

# MAKING TELEWORK WORK

# making
# *telework*
# work

## LEADING PEOPLE
## AND LEVERAGING TECHNOLOGY
## FOR HIGH-IMPACT RESULTS

EVAN H. OFFSTEIN + JASON M. MORWICK

**DAVIES-BLACK**
an imprint of Nicholas Brealey Publishing
Boston • London

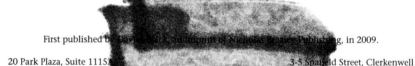

First published by Davies-Black, an imprint of Nicholas Brealey Publishing, in 2009.

20 Park Plaza, Suite 1115A                                3-5 Spafield Street, Clerkenwell
Boston, MA 02116, USA                                     London, EC1R 4QB, UK

Tel: + 617-523-3801                                       Tel: +44-(0)-207-239-0360
Fax: + 617-523-3708                                       Fax: +44-(0)-207-239-0370

www.nicholasbrealey.com

Special discounts on bulk quantities of Davies-Black books are available to corporations, professional associations, and other organizations. For details, contact us at 888-273-2539.

Printed in the United States of America

13 12 11 10 09     10 9 8 7 6 5 4 3 2 1

ISBN: 978-0-89106-252-3

**Library of Congress Cataloging-in-Publication Data**
    Offstein, Evan H.
    Making telework work  :  leading people and leveraging technology for high-impact results /
    Evan H. Offstein and Jason M. Morwick.
        p. cm.
    Includes bibliographical references and index.
    ISBN 98-0-089106-252-3 (hardcover)
    1. Telecommuting—United States. 2. Telecommuting. I. Morwick, Jason M. II. Title.
    HD2336.35.U6035 2009
    658.3'123—dc22
                                                                        2008037661
FIRST EDITION
First printing 2009

# CONTENTS

# PREFACE

We are in a time of great change. True to prediction, we live in a flatter, more competitive world, and the critical driver of this globalized small world is technology. On first blush, it may seem that the way to get ahead in this technical, fast-changing world is to become, well, more technical and fast-changing. We disagree. Both rigorous thought and research lay the foundation for our contrarian claim—the real way to benefit in this technology-rich world is to become a better leader and more sophisticated manager of technology, knowledge workers, and teleworkers. And in a snapshot, that's what this whole book is about: leading the real future workforce—the teleworkers. Conventional leadership theories and practice may have some applicability, but new strategies, techniques, and tactics are needed to lead teleworkers. So change is, indeed, needed. But it's not a change in technology; only a change in leadership can make telework work.

Many years have gone into writing this book. Some of what we report is personal experience. Other theories and applications come from interviews and observations. Some insight is derived from reading and research. In the spirit of protecting reputations of both people and organizations (and to more fluidly and potently convey a point), we took the liberty of altering and adjusting the times, names, places, and contexts in which the stories take place or when the principles were originally revealed. The bottom line is that all the stories are grounded in truth, but all are massaged lightly with some literary license to either protect reputations or more strongly and readily convey a point.

As authorities on this topic of leadership, we were amazed as we were preparing to write this book by the sheer amount of leadership dialogue devoted to yesterday, to the past. Conceptually, we're not sure how well that serves us in a business context, a nonprofit context, or a societal context. Rather, we feel that more leadership discussion needs to be directed toward the future. Frankly, we're not sure why there isn't more leadership debate and dialogue focused on the future; after all, the future is coming faster and faster these days. Reduced to a simple premise, leadership that fails to account for trends and technology of the future will no doubt be caught flatfooted in the present. And this is what makes this book, this leadership book, different. It has one eye on the present and another on the future. The future of telework is now, and its prevalence will only increase tomorrow. Our leadership principles, theories, tools, and strategies will help you today, tomorrow, and well into the future. We count this book as one of the few future-oriented leadership books on the market. Stay ahead of your competition, locally and globally, by embracing the forward-looking leadership tenets contained herein.

We'd like to say that leading teleworkers is easy stuff and that somehow lack of physical interaction makes leadership "less dirty." We can't and won't make that claim. In fact, we found unique challenges confronting leaders of teleworkers that oftentimes make their job harder, not easier. We do think we've answered many of these leadership challenges, but we'd be naive to think we've covered it all. And this is where you come in. With an eye to the future, we realize that any great leader and any great leadership approach are in a continual state of work-in-progress. For us, this book, and telework leadership to advance, we need your help and input. Send us your comments, questions, and feedback. We'd love to hear from you and may incorporate your insight and expertise into future thought regarding the leading and managing of teleworkers. In the meantime, let's do our best to make the future of leadership work—let's *Make Telework Work!*

# ACKNOWLEDGMENTS

We're not mathematicians, and there's no amount of fuzzy math could explain how this book came to be. On the left side of the equation, we had input from the Offstein contingent along with an equal amount of input from the Morwick contingent. The result, we feel, is a product that is much, much better than just the sum of its parts. Early on, we felt that our relationship and collaboration would make this a case where two and two equaled five, six, or seven, and we hope you'll agree. But we use the word "contingent" since a vast army of supporters helped either the Evan or Jason camp to persevere and improve. Very simply, this "book equation" could never have been solved through Jason or Evan alone, or even both together. Rather, we both relied on family, friends, colleagues, experts, and editors to see this product through to the end.

With that, we'd like to thank both of our families. On the Evan side that includes Laura, Madison, and Molly. On the Jason side, that includes Christa, Ainslee, and Maston. Writing a book is no easy feat and often requires sacrifices that extend way beyond the hardship of the author. Invariably, it is the family that sacrifices to see a book in print. We thank our families for the love, support, kindness, and just general agreeableness that they displayed over the nine-plus months it took us to write the book.

We can't and nobody should ever forget that this book is first and foremost about leadership, and we'd be remiss if we didn't pause to thank the leaders who have touched us—either directly or indirectly. We're not sure if this book could ever have been imagined, let alone written, without the strong web and network of past and present leaders that we've come across to hold it up. We offer thanks to the following: Alan Offstein, Patti Offstein, Jody Offstein, Al and Bernice

Offstein, Rick Morwick, Linda Morwick, Keri Smith, Sean Mikula, Brett Sciotto, Jeff Golan, Ed Sudzina, Mike Dugan, Art Callaham, Barb Buehl, Lee Fiedler, Danny Arnold, Del Pedew, Colleen Peterson, Pat Mifsud, Tony Wright, Rick Stafford, Bob Maricich, General Jerrold Allen, John Gould, Todd Uterstaedt, Doug Savage, Ahmad Tootoonchi, Michael Monahan, Kevin Govern, John Rhodes, Arthur Jones, Lowell Yarusso, John Spears, Kevin Shuba, Blair Tiger, Sara Gaba, Phil Daniels, Kerri Adams, Jonathan Gibralter, Tom Hawk, Quincy Crawford, Ralph Jordan, Mike Condrey, Tom Mastaglio, Bob Millward, Jack Hansen, Jason Schroeder, Teddy Williams, Toshi Desaki, Jeff Beamon, TJ Morrelli, Brian Joy, Larry McGhee, Jeanie Seifarth, Mark Sullivan, Barry Ronan, Bill Forster, Tom Grubbe, Tom Lamb, JoAnna Shore, Carol Gaumer, Debra Orner, Eric Hutchings, Gary Levenson, Devi Gnyawali, Terry Cobb, Donald Hatfield, John Winn, Kevin Carlson, Jeffrey Arthur, Steve Childers, Bill Stringer, "Rock" Roszak, Gloria Harrell-Cook, Ron Dufresne, David Harney, Claudia Ferrante, Scott Griffith, Don Battista, Cynthia Cycyota, Russ Haynie, John Hodson, Sue Head, Mike Min, Tom Dowdell, Al Moore, Lisa Cesnick, Bill and Robin Seddon, Alan and Carol Heft, John Walsh, Vic Martina, Brian Cameron, Nancy Rice, Tim Anderson, Chris Whitehurst, Gil Valadez, Joe Littley, Ed Deutschlander, Robert Vedra, Susan Bogan, Liza Dorsey, Shaun Bradley, Sean Carroll, Connie Kallback, Tammy Shockey, Nancy Rice, Mike Yankovich, Jeff Leischner, Maria Centeno, Jaume Pena, Keith Foster, Catherine Conley, Pauli Overdorff, and Allen Silverstein.

The publishing industry can be tough. Thankfully, we had Laura Lawson, senior acquisitions editor at Davies-Black, on our side. Laura Lawson, to us, is truly the gold standard of the publishing and book world. In our experience, if the industry would take a step closer to being like Laura Lawson, then it would be a different (and better) industry. She approached us and this project with such warmth, passion, kindness, and support that in spirit she deserves third authorship. We felt and saw her as an equal partner. Out of this entire process we wrote a book, and that's a great outcome. But maybe even a better outcome, for us, was finding a friend and colleague of the caliber of Laura. If we had to make this journey again, down the road, we'd ask Laura to sit shotgun to guide and mentor us through this process.

In closing, the authors' names on the covers of books are often a great misnomer and, in some cases, an injustice. At least in our case, we felt that the book only became a reality when our village and community of friends, family, and colleagues was there to help, assist, motivate, and support us. For that, we both owe debts that we know we'll never repay. Instead, we can only say thank you.

*Evan H. Offstein, PhD, SPHR*
Frostburg, Maryland
www.teleworkleaders.com
eoffstein@frostburg.edu

*Jason Morwick, MBA*
Orlando, Florida
www.teleworkleaders.com
morwickj@aol.com

# INTRODUCTION

*Everything should be made as simple as possible, but not simpler.*
**Albert Einstein**

Over two hundred years ago the Industrial Revolution forever transformed the working and social landscape. The advent of new technology increased productivity, expanded the knowledge of the individual, moved workers from the fields into the city, and changed the family structure. Today, the Information Revolution that began in the latter half of the twentieth century promises the same dramatic changes to the working environment.

The birth of the Internet Age signaled a change in how business is conducted, how customers interact with companies, and how employees engage with employers. Unfortunately, technology usually precedes social change. Like our ancestors witnessing the Industrial Revolution, we watch as many companies use new technology to do traditional business activities rather than truly reinvent how they do business or how their employees work. We have yet to maximize the capabilities of the technology that is already around us, and this is a failure in leadership. Many argue that technology is a game-changer, but leadership is the real catalyst—leadership to use technology in meaningful ways and to make telework work.

> *Making telework work is predicated on and largely a function of strong leadership.*

*Telework* is the framework of an idea—an approach to applying technology in both strategic and tactical ways to benefit organizations, teams, and individuals. The convergence of technology, accessibility of information, and how we think about personal interactions will change the way we work.

*Telework* refers to incorporating and optimizing technology to be more productive, to collaborate better, and to be more proactive. However, telework is not just about technology, it is about people. The manner in which people use technology in their work relationships is at the heart of making telework work.

This book is not about telecommuting. *Telecommuting* refers to replacing the daily commute with communication to the office. As Wikipedia states, "All telecommuters are teleworkers, but not all teleworkers are telecommuters." *Telework* is a much broader term that is about thinking and acting on a grander scale. Telework goes beyond just the "commute" part of a job, which involves little true work. Rather, telework changes jobs, changes the way we work, and, ultimately, changes organizations.

Specifically, telework is about employing technology to perform your job without the limits or boundaries of geography, time constraints, or the need for physical presence. Leaders can interact with their team members, workers can connect with their peers, and the organization can tap into the talent of all its employees more effectively than in traditional work arrangements.

Simple telecommuting, almost without exception, continues to be a failure on many levels. At the individual level, telecommuters often feel left out, ignored, under the radar. In our experience, teams aren't fond of their telecommuting members.[1] In the collective mind of the team, telecommuters shirk, don't pull their own weight, and are incapable of real contributions given their virtual status. Team members assume that telecommuters have it easy working from home while the remaining members do real (traditional) work. Teams with this mental model are, obviously, handicapped before they even begin to assign roles. For their part, organizations are confused on how to train, evaluate, and promote telecommuters—they are anomalies, outliers, people who don't easily fit within bureaucratic rules and processes.

It took decades to fully realize the benefits of the technology that brought the Industrial Revolution, but leaders today no longer have the luxury of time. The competitive advantage today goes to the leaders who can change their organization's business model faster and evolve their thinking more rapidly than the rest of the pack. We will show how leaders can integrate telework by influencing the people in their organization—peers, employees, and supervisors—to apply technology for optimal benefit.

## LEADERSHIP MAKES TELEWORK WORK

We stumbled upon a great contradiction during our research, one that is a core theme moving forward.

Despite the quantitative, technical, and exact science of telework, it is the art and qualitative nature of leadership that really makes technology work. We believe that the potential of technology is rooted not in bits and bytes but in something more abstract—great leadership.

For telework to actually work, individuals, managers, and organizations must address such issues as culture and climate change, strategic and personal change, training, communicating, influencing, environmental scanning, and listening. The same capabilities that make telework work are also the hallmarks of extraordinary leaders. So, as we go forward, we'll address both the leadership art and the management science of making telework work.

### Environment and Economics

Telecommuting is not a recent phenomenon. We can trace the concept back to the early 1970s, decades before the dot-com boom and explosion of telecommunications technology. Telecommuting has not reached its full potential and has failed to take hold because the concept emerged before the conditions were ideal. We believe that in regard to telework, the conditions are in place, and we are waiting on the concept to mature and evolve. That's where we come in.

#### A Failing Infrastructure and Long Commutes

The first major clue hinting at the rise of telework is the nation's failing physical infrastructure. Our roads, highways, and airports are overused and undermaintained. We simply cannot afford to rely on our physical infrastructure for even the most basic need—to get to work. According to *USA Today,* we spend 3.7 billion hours a year stuck in traffic—and that figure will continue to increase.[2]

We find ourselves living farther and farther from where we actually work. These variables swirl together to build a perfect storm—we live farther from work and spend longer on congested roads to get to work. The U.S. Census Bureau reports that the average daily commute is just over twenty-four minutes, one way.[3] New Yorkers have the highest commute times, with an average of approximately forty minutes, with many spending ninety minutes or more getting to work. People of Chicago, Newark, Philadelphia, and Los Angeles are not far behind.

With a knowledge-based economy like ours, time is indeed money. It is cold, hard cash, and leaders are leaving a ton on the table as they let themselves and their employees waste away in cars during a commute. The New Yorkers' forty-minute daily commute is the equivalent of eight working weeks per year. Couldn't the commute time be productive time? We think so, and telework can help us get there.

### A Growing Technology Infrastructure

Ironically, just as our physical infrastructure seems to be abandoning us, our information technology infrastructure has never been better. In most cities now, you can find Wi-Fi areas or hot spots that allow you to connect on the go from wherever you are. We have enough optical fiber underground, and now under our oceans, to facilitate ultra-fast data, voice, and video transfer. Only a couple of years ago, YouTube, Vonage, and other business models predicated on speedy data transfer would have been unthinkable. Now, they are both commonplace and affordable.

*The decline of our physical infrastructure will force many of us into telework.*

Along with an enhanced fiber backbone, computing power has dramatically improved while simultaneously getting smaller. What we mean by "getting smaller" is that advanced computing functions can now be found on mobile devices. When coupled with the improvements in IT infrastructure, we are seeing more and more mobile devices performing rather sophisticated computing functions.

For telework to really work, we found that participants need a floor of familiarity with both the hardware and software—what we call *mainstreaming*. Mainstreaming is occurring at a faster rate. iPhones, mobile phones, PDAs, and BlackBerrys are now commonly found in the executive suite as well as your daughter's bedroom. Without this basic familiarity and comfort among the general populace, telework cannot work. Fortunately, it exists here—and elsewhere, as we see mobile phone service extended to even the poorest and most rural parts of India.

### Environmental Benefits and Cost Savings

We can thank Al Gore for providing a global push for telework. The real watershed for the environmental and corporate partnership came after the release of Gore's movie, *An Inconvenient Truth*. This movie helped shape the economic and national agenda to ward against global warming. A chief global warming contributor, of course, is carbon emissions. Cars, planes, and office buildings release carbon into the atmosphere, both directly and when their sources of energy are prepared for use. Believe it or not, office buildings account for almost 40 percent of U.S. carbon emissions and 70 percent of energy use, according to the U.S. Green Building Council.[4] A 40 percent improvement in space utilization within a 100,000-square-foot office building is the equivalent of pulling 560 cars off the road for a year. Social responsibility is a core principle for many leaders, and embracing telework is another way to further this belief.

To the extent that telework can reduce unnecessary trips in either cars or planes or even reduce reliance on office buildings, it offers an attractive mechanism for reducing carbon emissions. Considering that organizations are placing this issue front and center in their strategic corporate social responsibility plans, telework should gain enhanced support from a crowd not usually associated directly with business nor technology—environmentalists.

Carbon emissions aside, the cost savings of telework should be attractive to any leader. According to a recent poll commissioned by Harris Interactive, U.S. workers waste an estimated $4.3 billion in energy costs per year, not to mention the resulting 32 million tons of $CO_2$ emissions associated with this energy consumption.[5] However, telework offers many other tangible benefits to the organization: reducing relocation costs of new employees, corporate real estate investment, recruiting costs, and absenteeism costs, to name just a few. Sun Microsystems, as an example, uses a flexible office space concept that allows workers to use office space when needed, and work off-site otherwise. Over 56 percent of Sun employees work without a traditionally assigned office.[6] In terms of IT and real estate cost reduction, the company has saved over $387 million.

Organizations and employees alike have an opportunity to save money through telework considering the ever-increasing cost of oil. Many scoffed a few years ago, when brokerage firm Goldman Sachs predicted the cost of oil at over $100 per barrel. In 2008, the average cost per barrel spiked to approximately $150. Although the current cost is well below that amount, it's not hard to imagine Goldman Sachs prediction of a super-spike to $200 per barrel in the not-so-distant future.[7] This equates to approximately $6 a gallon for the gas used by commuters and increasing energy costs for organizations.

*IT infrastructure, software, and hardware set the stage for telework to work. The variables holding us back are human, not technical; we need to look at our own leadership to make telework work.*

## The Business Benefits of Telework

Until now, our arguments have centered largely on the premise that you have to change, that you have to embrace telework. If you don't, you'll miss a large part of the workforce that supplies the team or the company its lifeblood of talent. If you don't embrace telework, you could also lose ground to your rivals. But the real rationale for embracing telework is not fear but opportunity. No question, telework provides real and potential competitive gains that are difficult to match.

### Gains in Productivity

Leaders or organizations that make telework work will see productivity gains that, until now, were unimaginable. To start off, telework enables a group or team to work twenty-four consecutive hours—as opposed to eight.[8]

### Talent, Talent Everywhere

From project management to human resources, truly great organizations compete by acquiring, building, and deploying talent. Until now, talent was confined by geography. The quality of work a team or company could deliver was constrained, at least in part, by the supply of

**THE ROLLING TWENTY-FOUR-HOUR WORK DAY**

One company we learned about was up against a deadline. The team in New York worked on the project for ten solid hours before sending it out to some teammates in California, who worked on the project for three or so hours before sending the project to Japan. The engineers in Japan worked the project over before sending it to some contacts in Europe. Technicians in Europe fine-tuned the project before sending it back to New York as the sun was rising there. Obviously, soft skills and great communications need to be in place before engaging in such a project. That's not the point here, though. By working with technology, the team was able to work on a project for twenty-four consecutive hours. Instead of taking three separate business days to complete, the team reduced time to delivery by 66 percent by sending electronic files across the globe.

talented individuals willing to live in the vicinity of the physical plant or office space. Geography is much less of a factor when we make telework work. A central human resource principle is to find, secure, and retain the best talent available. With telework, your labor pool is now global and you can scour the globe for talented workers who can contribute from miles away.

*Telework is directly and positively related to employee productivity.*

When a sick patient enters the Montgomery County Emergency Room (outside Blacksburg, Virginia) at 2 a.m. with kidney stones, telework reveals some of its power. Rather than waking a local urologist—of which there are precious few—a technician and nurse will administer a CAT Scan or renal ultrasound and send the files electronically to a urologist in Melbourne, Australia—saving time while securing talent that would otherwise be unavailable in southwest Virginia.[9]

### A Special Kind of Talent

In our discussions with several executives, we've heard that telework is also fair and reaches demographics that are immensely valuable but for some reason unable to commute. One such group is the disabled. The

Americans with Disabilities Act (ADA) is a civil rights law that prohibits most forms of discrimination based on disability. Furthermore, the ADA requires a firm to make accommodations for a disabled employee as long as the company does not face "undue hardships." In the past, these undue hardships have included such things as modifying work schedules, acquiring special equipment or modifying existing equipment, providing qualified readers or interpreters, or making desks and facilities wheelchair accessible. Telework is a win-win for both sides. The disabled employee can work in a home environment that is more comfortable and already modified to meet the employee's personal needs. The organization benefits by tapping into this talented and dedicated demographic without large capital outlays for costly physical modifications.

*Talent and telework are closely related. Telework allows previously unimaginable access to talent.*

*Telework can tap into labor markets that would otherwise be difficult to reach.*

### Economies of Scope and Scale

Among the early adopters of telework-type strategies are our nation's universities—a bunch often criticized for embracing the status quo. Perhaps few other industries have latched on to telework as much as academe. Leading the foray into telework or teleteaching environments are state universities, which have seen their state funding stagnate or dwindle. With telework, economies of scale and large efficiencies are often realized. Several applications and platforms allow a professor to create groups, assign forums to discuss topics, and administer remote and timed quizzes—all online and without physical interaction. Not confined by a brick-and-mortar classroom and its physical limitations, such as square footage per desk, the online tools open many possibilities. We've seen cases where a professor could only fit twenty-five students into a cramped classroom but could engage double that during an online class. In academe, we also see the professors being teleconferenced to many different classrooms at one time. Like academic institutions, most organizations would like lower overhead costs and greater access

*Telework promises enormous cost savings from economies of scope and scale.*

to markets—both labor and customer markets. Telework can provide just that.

### Hedging Against Risk

It is sad that we must bring up this last reason as a rationale to embrace telework. Telework allows both employees and organizations to hedge against risk. In the face of natural disasters such as Hurricane Katrina or man-made disasters such as the 9/11 terrorist attacks, telework allows for effective decentralization of activities. Knowledge, activities, and both human and financial capital tend to reside in the same space—in terms of time and location—in centralized models of operation. In this day and age, centralization is a risky venture. Telework allows us to spread our risk over and across people and locations.

The lessons offered by Katrina offer remarkably simple and straightforward evidence of the power of telework. Although a vast majority of people joined the exodus from New Orleans, critical and valuable work continued between those who left and those who stayed via telework arrangements.

Tulane University offers nuanced insight on how telework can work.[10] Tulane experienced tremendous physical damage during Katrina. Students, faculty, and staff dispersed. Scott Cowen, Tulane's president, established an emergency response team that relocated to Houston, Texas. From this location, several hundred miles from his traditional office in New Orleans, Cowen led a virtual crisis response plan and strategic rebuilding plan virtually via e-mail, cell phone, and common Web site platform utilization. What's more, several universities thousands of miles away from Tulane offered online credit programs so that displaced students would not fall behind in their coursework

*Telework is one of the greatest hedges against risk— both individually and organizationally. It is the ultimate diversification strategy.*

The Wall Street Journal (WSJ) offers another example. The prestigious newspaper used an editor's home, freelance journalists, and technology to put out an issue on September 12, 2001—a day after the attacks. By using remote, but basic, technologies such as e-mail and publishing software, the WSJ continued publication; it has been more than a hundred years since the WSJ missed a publishing date. WSJ Headquarters was located in the World Trade Center complex only feet from the collapse of Tower 2. When we examine how Tulane and *The Wall Street Journal* survived and even prospered while other organizations failed, the conclusion is clear. These organizations made telework work because they were prepared to adopt it. And being prepared is a leader's responsibility.

## IN THIS BOOK

We've tried to come up with a simple way to convey what is required to make the leap from using technology to benefiting and integrating technology at both the individual and organizational level. Every primary concept in our telework framework showed up time and again when we examined success stories. Here then is an overview of our discussion of the journey to make telework work.

**Chapter 1: The Leader as Conductor.** We were surprised, shocked really, to arrive at the realization that personal and organizational leadership is the key driver for making all telework work. However, it is not the traditional type of leadership; telework demands a special kind of leader—more of a symphony conductor. The leader-as-conductor concept suggests that leaders do as much listening as speaking, communicate well, remain flexible, and improvise when necessary. Just like symphony conductors, telework leaders are particularly skilled at seeing how pieces fit together to produce harmony.

**Chapter 2: The Leader's Decision-Making Process: Balancing Strategy, Tactics, and Technology.** The leaders who made telework work approached the process with equal parts strategy and tactics—they were stractical, if you will. Here we draw direct parallels between teleworking and the strategy behind the art of culinary fare. For instance, a restaurateur must plan months in advance and integrate multiple functions such as service, operations, feedback, and evaluation. Behind it all is a leader's disciplined, organized planning process that triggers several individual and team-related decision-making activities that make people come back for seconds.

**Chapter 3: How Leaders Create the Organizational DNA That Makes Telework Successful.** It may be a tough idea to confront, but without computers we would be in the dark about a very important topic—us. It was only with the advent of super-fast microprocessors that we were able to map the human genome, essentially the unique DNA sequence that makes us what we are. Without computers this task would be impossible to undertake. But technology needs us, too. In this chapter, we unlock the importance of core human resource strategies for recruiting, selection, training, performance evaluation, and compensation and benefits that seem to correspond with successful teleworking activities.

**Chapter 4: Leading Telework Teams in the Virtual World.** The notion of teams has achieved almost iconic status in management today. This entire chapter is devoted to telework teams not so much because they contribute to telework success as because poor telework team behaviors almost invariably lead to failure. For these reasons, we review the basic functions, stages, and conditions for optimum telework teams. Teams fit into a "meso" space between individuals and organizational policies. It shouldn't come as a surprise that there are specific activities that leaders can do along with some tailor-made organizational policies that can help make telework teams succeed.

**Chapter 5: Leadership: The Catalyst for Creating a Telework Culture.** Every organization has a culture. Leaders cultivate and grow an organization's culture to influence and reinforce behaviors. Some cultures don't support any technology. Many leaders grow cultures that barely support telecommuting. In this chapter, we describe what a telework culture looks like and juxtapose it with a culture fixed on traditional work arrangements. We discuss what leaders at all levels can do to help influence their organization's culture and advance change.

**Chapter 6: Accelerators: Tiny Leadership Variables with High Impact.** A company can implement all the conditions and major variables that should make telework work, and still see telework fail. The truth is, sometimes we all need a spark to mobilize dormant resources or abilities. The same can be said for making telework work. Here, we unlock several of the small variables—the leader accelerators—that seem to be particularly instrumental in making the bigger picture a reality. Don't overlook these little nuggets; time and again, they deliver sizable results.

**Chapter 7: Leadership Mistakes and Pitfalls.** In this chapter, instead of telling you what to do, we tell you what not to do as you make telework work. From poor planning to information overload to ignoring workers in traditional work assignments, a variety of pitfalls could spell disaster for your telework campaign if you fail to address them.

**Chapter 8: The Future Work Environment.** We wrap up with a look at trends and their likely impact on teleworkers and leaders. This conclusion is meant, of course, to encourage you to think about the changing work environment and how you can make telework work for competitive advantage.

We invite you to join us in transforming how work is done. Give it a try. We offer everything here based on personal experience or research. It is for you to try. We welcome any and all feedback. Be sure to visit us at www.telework leaders.com to join in and contribute to the telework dialogue.

# THE LEADER AS CONDUCTOR

*You do not lead by hitting people over the head—
that's assault, not leadership.*
**Dwight D. Eisenhower**

In 1982, Tom Peters and Robert Waterman released their landmark book *In Search of Excellence.* One of the popular concepts publicized in their study of Hewlett-Packard was a leadership tactic known as management by walking around (MBWA). The notion referred to management's proactive interaction with employees. Many took this idea literally. The good managers, one would reason, physically interacted with their staff through in-person meetings, impromptu visits, or some other face to face contact. The physical interface boosted morale, made communication more efficient, created a bond of trust, and encouraged greater collaboration . . . or so the argument went.

But what happens if your team members are hundreds (or thousands) of miles away in different time zones, actual in-person meetings are rare, and the main means of communication is e-mail or instant messaging with the occasional conference call?

One HR analyst at a midsized company told us, "We have a telecommuting policy and offer our employees the option, but hardly anyone takes advantage of it. Everyone is too afraid of how they will be perceived."

"I couldn't do it," recalled one successful Atlanta businessman. "I worked remotely for two years, and struggled the entire time. I needed to go back and work in an office."

"How do I know my people are doing what they are supposed to? I'm not sure I can motivate them without [physically] being around them," said another manager.

Can leadership work with no geographic boundaries or time constraints? Does leadership exist in the virtual world? Plausible as those questions seem, it turns out that leadership is the first and most important component to making telework work. And that is the key reason why cases in which telework has actually worked are so hard to find.

## THE CONDUCTING LEADER

In each and every case where telework works, great leadership is involved. Unfortunately, the corollary is equally relevant: In cases of failure something is conspicuously absent—great leadership.

Contrary to conventional wisdom, we don't believe technology should be managed. Rather than being *managed,* technology and telework arrangements should first be *led.* Moving beyond management, we also noticed that not just any type of leader would do. Hollywood often portrays leaders as large and in charge: vocal, autonomous, directive, authoritative, and even combative. But telework demands a different leadership approach. We were at a loss to classify, model, or label this leadership approach until our wives dragged us to a symphony concert. With the force of a crescendo, we then knew—telework needs a leader akin to a symphony conductor. The metaphor seems to hold. In cases where organizations were unable to make telework work, they suffered from the liability of having leaders who were not conductors.

## THE PROGRAM ELEMENTS

The world's best conductors realize that they have a choice in what is played and in what order. They don't take this notion of choice lightly, and they seem to grasp almost intuitively that this choice can either make or break a performance. We sensed the same type of implicit understanding when we talked to leaders who made telework work.

At the heart of this issue is the need to match market demand, whether that is internal or external demand, with internal capabilities. If there is no fit between these forces, then telework may be handicapped.

Listen to Beethoven's Third Symphony. Often referred to as the Eroica, which is Italian for *heroic,* this symphony is regarded both as one of Beethoven's best works and as one of the most difficult and challenging symphonies for any orchestra to play. When it is done well, you don't hear or see the difficulty, the rigor, the practice, the skill that went into it. You just hear the piece. The effort to get all musicians on one sheet of music can be Herculean for a conductor. The best conductors know it is not a simple decision to choose this piece. They first do an internal assessment of their orchestra's capabilities. When considering launching into this musical project, they ask the following questions:

- Are my musicians skilled enough as individuals to pull this off?

- Are my musicians skilled enough as a team to pull this off?

- If not, do we have the time to train to perform this to a high standard?

- Are there traps beyond just lack of skills or abilities, such as personalities, that would prevent this performance from succeeding?

- If so, can I remove these traps?

Conductors-as-leaders ask these very questions, and if they can't come to answers they're comfortable with, the show doesn't go on.

When approaching a telework arrangement, leaders should grab the conductor's baton and ask those same questions. Telework arrangements are a lot like symphonies—they differ in complexity and commitment. As you assess demand, you need to ask if your workforce or your team has the skills, abilities, commitment, and time to learn and engage this new technology arrangement. If the answer is no, wait until they can or choose a different score to play. Remember, playing the wrong song at the wrong time poorly is a recipe for disaster.

*Examine the fit between internal and external demand for technology with internal skills, capabilities, and commitment.*

## A THOUGHT EXPERIMENT

Picture yourself as a manager of a small team of project managers in a manufacturing company. Your project managers are charged with examining various internal processes and leading process improvement efforts. Although the company's plants are scattered across the country, your team works from cubicles that surround you in the company headquarters site. You have just interviewed the best candidate for one of the open requisitions on your team, but she lives on the other side of the country, and she has no intention of moving. To add to your headache, one of your top performers is requesting a more flexible schedule, to work from home at least several days a week to balance his current family issues. You could potentially lose him completely if accommodations aren't made.

As you stare into your monitor, one of your team members stops by with an interesting proposal. What if you disperse the entire team across the plant network? Several of the team members would gladly relocate and most would be open to the idea. He also suggests a flexible work schedule allowing people to work from home.

"No way" is your immediate gut reaction. But you quickly realize your response is out of fear. You've never done this before. As you take a step back, you start to think about your team. All of them are experienced professionals accustomed to working autonomously, and there is no need to monitor their daily activities.

The business case makes sense. Having the project managers engaged more closely with plant management may increase satisfaction among your internal stakeholders and produce better results. Plus, you will be able to pick up the number one candidate for your current open position and will maintain or even boost the productivity of the employee who is requesting a more flexible work arrangement. Sure, more consideration is needed before you jump into this new plan, but you have already begun your internal assessment.

## THE CONDUCTOR AS COMMUNICATOR

Harkening back to the conductor metaphor, great leaders make tele-work work by getting employees to play off the same sheet of music—or in the case of telework, to work off a common platform. We don't mean platform in a technology sense; we are referring to clear, open, disciplined, and deliberate communication. You'll notice that we will discuss communication throughout the following chapters as it's a key ingredient to making telework work.

### SWITCHING HORSES IN MIDSTREAM—
### THE ROLE OF COMMUNICATION

A large mid-Atlantic state university used a homegrown, internally de-signed e-mail platform. The four hundred faculty and staff and many of the six thousand students had used this unique, idiosyncratic e-mail platform for the better part of their professional and academic lives. For-get that the e-mail platform was a running joke in the greater academic community. It had limited portability, was full of bugs, and had none of the basic enhancements now commonly found in an e-mail program—a calendar function or rolodex and contact function, for example. To say that this e-mail program was primitive is an understatement. Finally, on a Friday in May 2005, the IT department pulled the plug; on the fol-lowing Monday, the university switched to Microsoft Outlook.

Pandemonium ensued. For about seventy-two hours, this univer-sity contemplated calling in the National Guard. Sit-ins, complaints, and calls for resignations spread like wildfire. The reason? The university had switched from its old, outdated, and damn near comical e-mail platform to one that was about a thousand times better. This change became a call to arms because senior university officials failed to ex-ercise a basic tenet of great leadership—communicate. They solved a technology problem and plunged into a human problem. A leadership problem.

## Ensuring People Understand Why

Getting a symphony orchestra on the same page of music isn't that much different from getting a department to embrace new software. What people want is the answer to the *why* question. They want to know why they are switching platforms, why they are using new back-office software, why they are shunning hard drives and CD-ROMs in favor of Web-based applications. Whatever the job, whatever the task, people tend to go crazy when they don't understand why they are doing it. It is the leader's task to answer and then communicate the *why* question. Refer to that university that decided to change e-mail platforms over a weekend. Most people would not have raised such hell if they just understood why they had to switch. Without the answer to the *why* question, employees begin to use their imagination to generate their own answers to the *why* question.

> *The launching point for making telework work is to communicate.*

> *Answering the **why** question may be the single most important responsibility of a leader.*

## Five Fringe Benefits

One astonishingly successful IT manager we know embraced a practical approach in dealing with the *why* question. Whether it was a hardware or software change or enhancement, this IT manager would draw up a list she titled "Five Fringe Benefits." This list answered the *why* question by showcasing how adopting a certain technology would make the person, team, department, or entire firm more efficient or make the person, team, department, or entire firm more effective. Ideally, the new technology and work arrangement should do both—make employees or work units both more efficient and more effective.

Consider the earlier scenario that involved a proposal to decentralize a team of project managers. Will the proposed change in work structure make the team more efficient? More effective? The following example provides the sort of information that needs to be considered.

Going through the *why* exercise has promising effects for both the employees and the leader. For sure, it gets the leader to think more deeply about the technology–work relationship. In fact, if a leader can't

**APPLYING EFFICIENCY AND EFFECTIVENESS**

After doing some more digging, you discover that most of your team members commute approximately forty minutes each way. Surfing the Web, you find a myriad of surveys and studies that indicate those working from home are more productive, and correlated to their productivity they work more hours. You also get the team's feedback and find that the majority of their meetings, with the exception of your weekly staff meeting, are conference calls or Web meetings. Therefore, you reason, you're not necessarily losing any productivity from lack of face to face interactions because the team is already working virtually from a few cubicles away. You are confident that the new arrangement answers the question of efficiency.

But what about effectiveness? You know the opinion of plant management and how they view the corporate folks at headquarters. You solicit their feedback about this idea and receive positive feedback about the potential increased interaction with the project managers. If the project managers are closer to the plants, they can get to their internal customers more often and can see (and fix) problems firsthand.

As you prepare to meet with your boss to present the new working proposal, you have your list of five fringe benefits: Productivity is likely to increase across all the individual team members. You will be able to accommodate your top performer who needs the flexible work schedule and not lose him. You will be able to hire top talent that is currently not available in your location. Plant management will be happier because they may have increased interaction with the project managers and the negative "us versus them" perception will recede. Project results may improve due to more collaboration between the project managers and plant managers.

answer the *why* question in five simple sentences, then the operative question becomes, Why do it at all? Also, if the five fringe benefits are abstract, unquantifiable, or just too complex to put into simple language, then the leader must reflect about moving forward. In essence, the *why* exercise may benefit the leader more than the followers because it focuses leaders on the truly important questions and forces them to answer before moving ahead. Remember—embracing, integrating, or launching a new technology should never be taken lightly. There's no need to change just to change. All technology–work arrangements must be based on a rationale of benefits that support the move. One successful CEO that we interviewed offered this last piece of counsel: The value of the five fringe benefits should outweigh expected financial and time-related costs by a factor of five before it is desirable to move forward.

**Answer the why question for both your own benefit and for those you lead.**

## Communicate, Communicate, Communicate . . . and Communicate Again

A good friend of ours is a marketing consultant for small and entrepreneurial businesses. One day over lunch he was telling us that he explains to his clients that it takes at least thirteen "touches"—encounters with an idea—for a potential customer just to *hear* a message. It takes another thirteen touches for that potential customer to *listen* to that message. Then it takes another thirteen touches for that customer to make a buying decision with that particular sales pitch in mind. In summary, according to our marketing friend, it takes thirty-nine interactions via radio, print ads, the Internet, and TV before one of his firms really reaches a potential customer.

While you may not need to go to such lengths, we advise you to heed the spirit of this message. After you come to grips with why telework is important and beneficial, the next question to ask is, *How* do I get this message across? The first answer is the sheer frequency of exposure. Another way to think about this is to view communication as a contact sport; the more times you contact or touch the employees affected by a telework arrangement, the more likely they will hear, listen, and adopt the rationale.

**Leaders can never over-communicate. Get out there and do it.**

To make sure that everyone who needs to be touched is indeed touched, communicate according to this mantra—*once, twice, up, down, left, right, written, verbal*. When a message is communicated once, twice, up the organization, down the organization, to departments on the left, departments on the right, and via both written and verbal media, the *why* is more likely to stick. And that's important, as answering the *why* question only to yourself or to a small number of insiders does more harm than good. Leaders who want to make telework work move from answering the *why* question to answering the *how* question. Specifically, leaders ask, *How* do I get the message across to all directly and indirectly affected personnel in a manner that will stick?

## One Size Doesn't Fit All

The truth about communication is that people process information differently. Expert research suggests that the medium in which a message is carried affects the way people process it. For this reason, it is okay to mix it up. Get your message across via personal and face to face communication. Look at using bulletin boards. Mass phone announcements. Blogs. E-mail blasts. Podcasts. Your company intranet. This simple notion of diversifying your communication media produces enormous benefits; it allows you to reach more people since some people respond differently to various media. If you were only to use e-mail, you'd be apt to miss the vast group of people who prefer to process information via the human voice—whether that is telephone or face to face communication.

Related to this message, remember that the *why* statement may need to be altered depending upon the targeted audience. This is true for implementing any new work structure or technology. For example, the rationale for choosing new back-office accounting software will be different for an accounts receivable clerk from what you need to present to an IT worker. Another useful imperative is to tailor the complexity of the language to the specific audience. A leader may want to go into detail regarding a new enterprise software platform that will be used by program managers. However, the leader may tone down the complexity of that message when speaking to a union foreman, who may only tangentially use this new platform. A shrewd communicator seems to implicitly understand that one size doesn't fit all and that some care and deliberation may be needed to craft different messages depending on the stakeholders involved. If it seems that we

> *Great leaders know that one message never fits all.*

are getting into excruciating detail here, it is because we are. Communication is *that* important in making telework work.

## THE KEY PLAYERS: RACI

After *how,* you need to address the question of *who* is properly involved in your communications. Many of the best consulting firms in the world, from Bain & Company to Maine Pointe to McKinsey, use some variant of the RACI approach (pronounced *ray-see*) to facilitate disciplined and operational excellence within a firm's leadership group. While these world-class consulting firms use RACI methodology, the approach is not proprietary and is free for all to use. More than anything else, RACI helps with the *who* question. When used properly, it facilitates an understanding of roles, responsibility, and ultimately accountability. As such, it serves to enhance both communication and leadership.

### Responsible

"R" individuals may not own the task, but they are *responsible*. This group assists the person accountable for achieving the desired outcome, whether that is a program, process, or task. This level of responsibility can and often is shared among two or more people. Their degree and level of responsibility is determined by the accountable person, the owner of the function.

### Accountable

Next are the "A" people. The "A" in the RACI approach stands for the person *accountable* for the program or task. This individual is ultimately accountable for delivering the product, program, or service on time and at an agreed-upon level of quality. Typically, only one A person is assigned a process, task, and function. Of course, the value in establishing an A person is to clearly highlight where the buck stops. Think about it another way—if everybody owns a task or program, then nobody really does. Shared ownership can diffuse responsibility and accountability. And in truly top-shelf organizations, roles, responsibilities, and levels of accountability are clearly defined and articulated.

## Consulted

The "C" stands for the people who need to be *consulted*. Whether you're a conductor or a leader trying to implement a telework arrangement, this group is particularly important. A conductor just doesn't choose a score independently. More often than not, the conductor will seek counsel, advice, and just generally consult with experts within the orchestra such as the first violin—the musician regarded as most skilled in playing the violin. Leaders wishing to make telework work should also consult and bring their own experts into the process before a final decision or action is taken. Consultation generates two particular benefits as it applies to telework. First, the leader gets important feedback and subject matter expertise from valuable sources within the organization. When this feedback is taken seriously, the final telework arrangement is usually better. Second, and maybe just as important, being consulted gives people a stake in the results; it makes them stakeholders. This empowering relationship generates commitment and support within the larger group when the decision and actions are finally executed. Leaders facing a technology change or enhancement should think carefully about whom they should consult. And again, don't overlook the consulting aspect of the RACI methodology—it provides real substantive contributions both technically and culturally.

One of the more scientific and effective ways to consult before a decision is made is to send out a survey. Surveying is now mainstream. You see it every day when you watch CNN or log on to ESPN.com. Surveying can be as simple or as complex as needed. Some great Web-based tools such as SurveyMonkey.com or Zoomerang.com make it possible to build, distribute, and collect information on a survey within minutes. Political pollsters, businesses, and governments are obsessed with surveys because they want hard numbers to bolster policy and decisions. Knowing this, use surveys to get more people involved quickly, but also to provide some numeric evidence behind the decision-making process.

## Informed

Finally, you have the "I" component. "I" stands for people who need to be *informed* of the decision and progress of the overall technology initiative. The rationale goes back to why that university almost had to shut down after it switched e-mail systems—people weren't informed. They felt a mixture of confusion and disrespect and reacted with fury, all because they weren't given the professional courtesy of being informed.

## Other Elements

Many variants of the RACI model can be found on the Internet. Two popular variations include RASIC or RASCI. Depending on the version, the "S" can mean either *support* or *signatory*. Acting in a supporting role, the person or organization may provide resources to support the task or assignment. Using the "S" as signatory, this refers to the person who has to sign off or approve the deliverable. Different from the person assigned as the accountable individual, the signatory may only participate as the formal approver and not necessarily be involved in the execution of the task. Regardless of which designation is used, the intent is to give those using this tool the flexibility to include key stakeholders that may not be covered by the basic RACI model.

*Provide clarity of roles and responsibilities by using a RACI matrix.*

It may help to put the RACI information into a leader matrix. That way, it's easy to see who owns, is responsible for, or should be consulted or informed for any given technology task or project. Realize that this RACI tool serves to clarify and crystallize individual roles and responsibilities. Given that most people don't like ambiguity or being left in the dark, this RACI matrix is tough to beat.

## THE AGENT OF CHANGE

Sports, music, politics, religion, food, dance: All are societal conventions or customs. None are as closely tied to change as technology. Technology and the telework that it allows are at their most basic root about change and adaptation. This is a great paradox and one that we guarantee that leaders who try to bring telework to the table will encounter. The paradox is that to grow, survive, and live, we must—just as plants do—change. The quandary is that we are so resistant to change. Through habits, ritual, and just a general dislike of anything different, as a species we hate to change.

As part of doing research for this book, we conducted an informal survey where we queried people about their Internet usage. Almost all of our fifty or so respondents informed us that they visit no more than six Web sites on any given day and that those six most frequently visited Web sites hadn't changed in the last eighteen months. For example, one individual reported going to the following Web sites every day: ESPN.com, CNN.com, VT.edu, MySpace.com, Yahoo.com, and eBay.com. It's amazing that given the immense choice—more than 40 million possible Web sites—typical individuals only visit six or so routinely and visit the same ones every day. The same thinking applies to how people get to work. There are probably at least ten different ways for a person to get to work—each about the same distance, the same difficulty, and the same amount of time. But most of us stick to one, and we don't deviate. These are the forces of habit, resistance, and ritual leaders face as they try to implement telework arrangements. The tension is a serious one— most people favor inertia and the status quo, a position that if adhered to jeopardizes their very survival.

> *Great leaders deal with and drive change. Others fall victim to the status quo and inertia.*

Change is a major thread that weaves throughout our book. We spotlight the issue here for no other reason than that leaders who make telework work are those who are able to deal with, drive, and demand change. Time and again, leaders or organizations that fail to embrace and execute telework arrangements are victims—not victors—of change.

### MAKING CHANGE: TELEWORK FOR SALES

A common telework arrangement is that of sales force automation plat-forms. After all, sales is a commonsense arena in which to apply the telework concept. Most organizations don't want their sales reps sitting behind desks. Instead, for sales forces to be effective they need to be out in the field, out in the streets, making contacts and closing sales. Conservative industry analysis suggests that at least $3 billion a year is invested into sales force automation.[1]

Sales force automation (SFA) platforms fit squarely into this change-oriented dilemma. SFA platforms require that the salespeople input valuable data regarding their clients and possible customer leads. Ide-ally, this data helps a firm become more sophisticated in understand-ing and serving each customer. For instance, some SFA systems integrate this sales data with other highly interdependent functions such as marketing, customer service, and even manufacturing design. Take for example a scenario where customers are complaining about the packaging of a new drug—the packaging is too cumbersome for elderly patients to open. If these complaints and concerns are gathered via SFA platform by salespeople in the field, the information can be col-lected and combined with other agent comments. With some analysis, the pharmaceutical firm can see if this is a serious problem that affects many patients across many markets or is just a few isolated cases. If the problem is viewed as pervasive, manufacturing and logistics may pursue a redesign effort. None of this could occur without SFA and the telework arrangement. The tracking and customer service that accom-panies SFA should also lessen the burden on the salesperson of pick-ing up the phone or taking time away from the customer to perform basic customer service functions such as package tracking. From a CEO's vantage point, SFAs are beautiful and elegant; they allow the salespeople to focus on relationship-oriented activities that coincide with developing leads and closing sales—the very reason why these ex-troverted professionals were hired in the first place!

But salespeople generally hate SFAs. The challenge here is about communication and change. Salespeople resist SFAs largely because of fear. When salespeople hear *automation,* what they feel is a loss of control over how they do their jobs and also over their own client listings, which are gold for any salesperson. Walking in their shoes and listening, which is the most underrated component of communication, you may learn that salespeople think that SFAs will monitor their every move and that all valuable customer information will no longer be theirs but the organization's. Remember, salespeople tend to be fiercely independent and resist being monitored. They tend to work from home and work at their own schedule. Simply, many salespeople just view SFAs as intolerably intrusive and opposed to the very nature of their entire profession.

Breaking the barrier of resistance is necessary for telework to take hold and actually work. Effective leaders see technology adoption and change management as one and the same. Three key leadership activities are essential in enabling telework and defeating the forces of inertia and status quo: developing a sense of urgency, building networks of power, and celebrating success.

## Sense of Urgency

Above all else, we've seen that effective leaders create a sense of urgency behind telework initiatives. These types of leaders create an artificial burning platform that jolts individuals into choosing between adopting the technology or facing extinction. One case in point was a large distribution facility that was moving from printed labels to bar code scanners. To urge people into adoption, several leaders suggested that if this distribution center was not successful, they would fall to competitors and jobs could hang in the balance.

*Create a sense of urgency behind telework adoption.*

## Networks of Power

Telework advocates also grasp the importance of informal networks of power within their organization that could help or hinder telework arrangements.

"I shoot for the influencers," recalled one successful department head. "I know if I can win over the handful that help shape informal opinions and add grist for the rumor mill, I know I've won. I influence the influencers who, in turn, persuade everybody else. When done right, it makes my job quite easy."

*Build alliances and coalitions with informal power brokers. Influence the influencers!*

Leaders need to tap into and co-opt these informal networks. Hit them up early and make sure they're on your side as you try to make telework work.

## The Celebrator

We found conductor-like qualities that further upped the chances that telework would work. Specifically, these conductors would remove obstacles so as to make playing the new technology as painless as can be. Time and again, we saw telework conductors celebrate small victories. Intuitively, these master conductors seemed to understand and even anticipate that not everybody is going to learn the whole technology symphony at one time. In these cases, leaders-as-conductors celebrated the smallest victories.

*Remove obstacles early in the experience. Don't forget to celebrate the small victories.*

These mini-celebrations produced two special benefits. First, they raised individual and collective confidence that the telework initiative would indeed work. Second, they created some organizational momentum to encourage people to keep trying.

## THE POWER BROKER

In the course of writing this book we decided to interview some composers, musicians, and even a conductor to see if we were heading in the right direction, to see if our metaphor would hold. It did. Our conversations revealed an additional insight into the power of the best conductors. In both the short and long term, the most effective conductors used varying sources of power at just the right time.

To start it off, power is the tool that gets things done. Power, in its simplest definition, is the ability to influence others. When used judiciously, it can overcome inertia, negativism, and the status quo. What many don't realize is that power comes from a variety of sources, and not all sources are effective all the time.

Broadly speaking, most leaders reading this book enjoy several sources of power, including legitimate, reward, expert, referent, and coercive power. All are incredibly useful as they relate to making telework work.

## Legitimate Power

Legitimate power is the formal authority that comes with the leader's position within the hierarchy of the organization. The CEO of the company has greater ability to influence employees than a junior manager. Although we emphasize throughout this book the need to get senior leaders to support telework, we don't want to understate the legitimate power that all leaders possess. Whether a person is a vice president leading an entire department or a project manager temporarily leading a cross-functional team, all leaders have the ability to influence those around them.

## Reward Power

Reward power is a leader's ability to influence another's behavior through "carrots," or rewards. Remarkably, and counter to conventional thought, oftentimes rewards don't need to be astronomical. We know of one case where a university was having a rough time recruiting faculty to create online classes or virtual classrooms— another example of telework in the educational arena. After some time of limited success, the university offered free training classes at multiple and convenient times along with a $100 gift certificate for those who committed to teach one online course during the next semester. Within ten minutes of announcing this policy, the university had its ten volunteers. The better part of this story is that once the professors saw how well the online format worked for them, as well as for their students, the professors continued to sign up for future semesters. The $100 reward was just the spark they needed to sign up.

*Use carrots to motivate individuals to get behind telework.*

## Expert Power

Expert power is the ability to influence behavior because of specialized knowledge, expertise, or competencies. We were involved in one project where a firm was introducing a new knowledge management system. To get people on board, the firm brought in a leader in the field, a technologist from MIT, to sit down with the soon-to-be engineering group over a brown-bag lunch to answer their questions. Because this person with respected credentials and viewed as a world expert on knowledge management supported the idea, it was easier for the engineering group to do the same. Credentials matter. And they can tip the scales in favor of telework.

*For telework arrangements, consider bringing in an outside expert to speak regarding the project.*

## Referent Power

Often conductors rely on their referent power. Referent power is a leader's ability to influence thought and deed through nothing more than being admired, respected, or liked. Typically, referent power accrues to conductors who have led successful symphonies before or at other venues. In business as well, referent power usually involves a body of work or a track record of success. This is probably a common-sense take-away that applies to more than just telework initiatives. Any goal, project, or program is easier, better, and more fun when the person leading it is respected, liked, and admired. Pray for the success of any given program when the most hated person in the organization is driving its bus. Our guess is that there won't be too many passengers.

*People will charge through change barriers when they are being led by someone they respect.*

## Coercive Power

Finally, we come to coercive power. It may be politically incorrect to discuss this type of power. After all, it has fallen out of favor in our more egalitarian and empowered organizations. Despite this less-than-popular status, though, we did see evidence that coercive power works.

One telling example of how coercive power is used is through the "burning bridge"—as opposed to the burning platform—notion to create urgency. The metaphor of the burning bridge is rooted in military history and folklore. In this folklore, colonels would march their soldiers across the bridge over a deep ravine. Once across, the colonel would order the bridge burned. The lesson from that move is clear and unequivocal: there is no choice, no retreat, no surrender. There's no going back, and all who made it across will now fight to the death.

Yes, we know, it sounds quite melodramatic. But that's exactly what three Marquette business professors propose when it comes to the sales force automation platforms we discussed earlier. Professors Cotteleer, Inderrieden, and Lee suggest that when all else fails, make it mandatory. When leaders do this, they present the ultimate decision to those that follow: Follow now or get off. But choose one, because it is nonnegotiable. If you stay, you will be part of the telework initiative, because we are moving forward with it. Some may judge this as unfair and cruel. We view it as strong leadership that ultimately transfers the choice of staying or going to the follower or user.

*Burning the bridge is an option. Consider it as one. Never dismiss it out of hand.*

To many people, especially those not wearing conductor hats, telework is about cables, codes, software, hardware, bits, and bytes. We see it more as influencing, inspiring, communicating, and motivating. So, while many first see telework as about data or things, we—along with the conductors we saw and interviewed—know telework is first about people. Make no mistake, these conflicting perspectives cannot be any more different. And this difference is critical: It is the difference between telework working and telework failing.

# GUIDING PRINCIPLES

Throughout this chapter we have discussed the need for telework arrangements to be led rather than managed. Good leadership is the fundamental building block of all business engagements, and telework is no different. Remember that the leadership involved in making telework work may be slightly different from the mental image you have envisioned in other environments. We propose that the telework leader is one who can harmonize the efforts of others to reach organizational goals without the need for direct, authoritative control. At a minimum, we offer the following guiding principles to leaders to implement telework arrangements.

*Conduct an internal assessment.* Telework can be a challenge, and consideration is needed before launching into it. Although the concept is attractive to many, few can make it work successfully. Leaders should conduct an internal assessment of their team, department, or organization's capabilities. Chapter 3 takes this a step further and discusses a company's capabilities from a Human Resources perspective, and Chapter 5 describes ways to take the company culture into account.

*Communicate, communicate, communicate.* With any initiative, communication—clear, open, disciplined, and deliberate communication—is vital to success. Leaders have to get their teams on board and on the same page.

*Answer the why and how.* When developing a communication strategy, leaders should address two fundamental questions, the why and the how. The answer to how should take into account the frequency with which the message is generated, to what audiences, and by what medium. Remember that the more times you communicate to employees affected by a telework arrangement, the more likely they are to hear, listen, and adopt the rationale. Since people process information differently, the message may need to be altered to suit the targeted audience.

***Employ appropriate tools.*** Employ appropriate tools. Leaders can leverage various tools to aid them in the communication process. In this chapter, we offered two such tools, the Five Fringe Benefits (FFB) and RACI, but many others exist that have similar purposes. These tools can help create the business case for telework or ensure the right practices are engaged.

***Exercise change management.*** Closely linked to communication is change management. Working through barriers of resistance is necessary for telework to gain acceptance and ultimately become successful. Effective leaders vary their approach and employ multiple methods to change behavior. Whether it is celebrating small successes, creating a case through hard data, applying interpersonal skills, or even mandating certain decisions, the leader has a full repertoire of approaches to consider.

# 2

# THE LEADER'S DECISION-MAKING PROCESS: BALANCING STRATEGY, TACTICS, AND TECHNOLOGY

*It is our choices that show what we truly are, far more than our abilities.*
J. K. Rowling, *Harry Potter and the Chamber of Secrets*

Greyhounds are fast. But technology can slow them down, and slow them down it did. In the early 1990s, the storied bus company, Greyhound, launched a technology platform called TRIPS.[1] TRIPS was supposed to be an upgraded reservation and bus-dispatch system. Expectations were high as Greyhound poured about $6 million (roughly $30 million in today's dollars) into TRIPS. Unfortunately, TRIPS ruined many trips during its launch in 1993. Whenever Greyhound offered sale prices on bus fares, the system would crash. The users of this system, Greyhound booking agents, lost all confidence in it and even resorted to writing tickets by hand while customers waited in line and missed buses. The agents weren't the only ones losing confidence; ridership plunged 12 percent in one month. A couple of months and a $61.4 million loss later, the CEO and the CFO resigned. Many experts believe that TRIPS cost Greyhound dearly—nearing two decades after the TRIPS incident, Greyhound has failed to regain the market share it once owned.

## LEADING DECISIONS ABOUT TELEWORKING

What do bus trips have to do with telework? Everything. Whether an organization is implementing a new enterprise resource planning (ERP) system, a new collaborative technology application, or a telework arrangement, the factors for success (or failure) are the same. Leadership is not only about motivating or influencing people; it's also about making decisions, creating a vision, and delivering results. The Greyhound scenario is a telling one. It illustrates what can happen when leaders have the misfortune of following poor strategy with, even worse, poor execution. Ultimately, it is the leader, and the leader's decision-making process, that must bring all the parts together to create a meaningful whole.

Greyhound is certainly not alone. Many technology projects fail. Many are not completed on time or overrun the budget or fail to live up to expectations. In our research and interviews with managers, we found, unsurprisingly, that the success of telework, or of technology projects in general, had less to do with the technology and more to do with leadership. In our interviews, common reasons for project failure centered on familiar activities such as gaining executive support, developing clear goals or a plan, communicating effectively, or managing expectations. These elements are the responsibility of the leader and not necessarily dependent on any specific technology. In this chapter, we focus on two key success factors the leader must control and account for. To truly make telework work, leaders must straddle the divide between strategy and execution.

## "STRACTICAL" THINKING

We drew inspiration for this book from the reality around us. If the spark of creativity for the last chapter was a symphony, for this chapter it was a good friend of ours, Kevin, who had decided to forsake his life and open a restaurant. His personal entrepreneurial journey and the human dimension of technology as revealed in our research display many striking parallels.

**THE RESTAURATEUR'S LIFE**

Rocco DiSpirito was the star of the 2003 NBC hit reality show, *The Restaurant.* In an American Express ad that also promoted the show, Rocco famously remarked, "I'm a chef who already runs two restaurants in New York. Now, I'm opening a third on national television in a time when nine out of ten restaurants fail in the first year."

Eighteen months after our overworked, underpaid, and sleep-deprived friend launched his own restaurant (not on national TV), Kevin reflected on this brutal statistic. "The number one reason why restaurants fail is not lack of capitalization. It is the owner's inability to think stractically."

We paused. "Don't you mean strategically?"

"Nope."

We tried again. "You meant tactically, then. Right?"

"No. Great owners and great restaurateurs do both. They think strategically while simultaneously thinking tactically."

We thought we knew where he was going with this. He drove the point home.

"Think about it. Great strategy without execution is worthless. It is just ideas. But nailing the tactics, the operations behind a faulty strategy is equally dangerous. Definitely, you need both. You need a strong strategy. And you need to be good tactically to execute on that strategy."

Reflecting on the Greyhound case, the clarity of Kevin's insight seems profound. The bus company may have had a great technological concept, but it was lost in execution. Time and again, the crucial factor in both personal and organizational cases of making telework work was the leader's ability to think and act stractically.

A stractical mind-set as it applies to technology is really a study in duality. This mind-set can see both the short-term (tactical) and long-term (strategic) implications of the technology adoption. This mind-set can simultaneously visualize why the technology will make an impact (strategy) and the hardships that accompany deploying and executing the technology (tactics). When it comes to telework arrangements, a special mind-set is indeed needed. It is a mind-set that can reconcile the theory or strategic relevance of the new telework arrangement with the practice required to make it work. Stractical is the equal embrace of two notions that most people usually separate—theory and practice. The leader must grasp the big picture while still accounting for the details.

*In cases of making telework work, the leader has to think and act stractically.*

## TIME IS MONEY

The two key areas where stractical thinking manifests itself are money and time investments. Stractical thinking means that a leader can juggle the seeming contradiction between short- and long-term time horizons and big and small financial investments. Kevin, our restaurateur friend, is a prime example.

Early on, Kevin made a stractical decision regarding a type of enterprise application software available to restaurants. Instead of using a pad and pencil to take the customer's order, the waiters and waitresses use a handheld electronic device. The device populates a database so management can track customer preferences, staff performance, and inventory levels by the minute. And the information is transmitted wirelessly back to the kitchen so the cooks know exactly what the order is.

Kevin's stractical thinking surfaced as he contemplated making this technology investment before opening his restaurant. Stractically, Kevin knew the investment was a wise one. It would enable him to track performance in real time, judge how certain dishes were selling, and plan inventory better. Stractically, he knew the best time to implement this software was before the restaurant opened. To retrain his staff months down the road—after habits and procedures were set and established—could cause disruption in preparation and service. Understanding that consistency is the name of the game in the restaurant business, Kevin wanted to make all mistakes early and begin the learning curve sooner rather than later. Avoiding the risk of starting everything at once would have been a penny-wise and pound-foolish decision: an example of tactical-only thinking. Leaders think stractically. Kevin did, and his new restaurant is still in business today.

Teleworking requires financial investment too. What type of technology will the business rely on to keep everyone connected? How will workers be equipped and what support will be provided for them? Additionally, it requires intangible investments, such as determining how management practices may need to change to support teleworking. The leader must see the short- and long-term challenges and weigh them against the benefits of teleworking.

Kevin grasped that technology could provide attention to detail and that failure to attend to minute details in the restaurant industry is a recipe for strategic demise. It's a point worth hammering home. Don't think strategically about telework. Don't think tactically. Think stractically.

*Stractical thinking reconciles the tension between short- and long-term time frames and big and small financial outlays.*

## BETWEEN DEPENDENCE
## AND INDEPENDENCE

Leaders need to understand the true interrelatedness of technology and work. When leaders think stractically, they have a basic understanding of the theory of interdependence—the connections between technology and other personal and professional functions. Without this understanding, it is almost impossible to fully comprehend how technology transforms work. Technology and work aren't separate, independent entities. Rather, they are blended so tightly together that they are indistinguishable; they can't be teased apart. When this occurs, you've got interdependence. More important, you've transformed technology and work to the extent that telework now works. Thinking stractically for leaders is crucial because leading is *thinking* in our virtual, teleworking world.

Teleworkers rely on technology to get work done; however, too much dependence on anything, including technology, is never good. Consider cell phones, PDAs, and BlackBerry devices. In severe cases, we've seen true dependence on the technology—both physical and psychological. Dependence is usually followed by obsession—and at this point, technology, and not the user, is in control. On the other end of the spectrum is independence. Although independence means that an individual is free from support or aid, it can also mean that users are disconnected or organizational silos are created.

Sometimes even the smallest technology upgrades can impact all facets of work. One of the more entertaining stories we came across was that of a physician who after years and years of old-school traditional work arrangements decided to change.

### LEARNING TO CHANGE

From the beginning of his practice, this physician had served a population that could best be described as older, a touch less educated than the U.S. average, and in slightly poorer health than the norm. As years went by, patients were more and more likely to arrive at the office late and with the wrong paperwork. Meanwhile, front-office staff spent a good portion of the day calling patients with reminders of appointments. Since many patients couldn't hear too well, the staff would have to repeat the message time and again. Finally, the physician switched to scheduling software that called patients automatically. To the staff's relief, the automated system allowed the patients to replay the message over and over again if they didn't hear it the first time. The results were immediate and profound. Billing errors were halved since the patients brought in the right paperwork. Late appointments were reduced to fewer than one a day. Backlogs got processed more quickly and, ultimately, the doctor had more time with patients.

The physician's decision to implement the new software is similar to any leader's decision to launch a new technology or telework arrangement. The automated calling system had a ripple effect across the various functions and processes within the physician's office. A leader should be able to foresee the impact of such a decision on other business functions, systems, and processes.

Interdependence isn't always roses. It also has its challenges. When a technology platform goes wrong, all facets of work can be impacted. We don't dispute this worrisome fact. However, the important lesson here is that the merging of technology and work will almost always result in some form of interdependence.

> *Without exception, every case of telework working involves real interdependence.*

## PRESERVING ORGANIZATIONAL FLEXIBILITY

Stractical leaders know that one of the biggest benefits of blending technology and work is to provide flexibility. Of all the lessons and principles regarding telework, it is this notion of flexibility that leaders most often violate. Sadly, one of the more dominant themes to emerge as we reviewed cases of telework failure was that the technology did the exact opposite of achieving flexibility—it constrained the individual or organization. It is difficult to overstate the essential lesson for stractical leaders: Integrating technology into work arrangements should always enhance personal or organizational flexibility—never detract from it.

Technology can indeed constrain individuals and reduce their freedom to respond to the demands of daily work. Once the investment is made, technology quickly gets embedded into the entire fabric of the organization. And that's a chief culprit in making technology work against flexibility. Think of technology as a plant (not a weed) with deep, long, and powerful roots. Pulling up a plant like this can disrupt the entire garden. For instance, pulling up and yanking out a system such as the popular PeopleSoft personnel application is difficult because it impacts so many other functions—recruiting, staffing, performance evaluation, payroll, scheduling, vacation, benefits, and governmental reports related to diversity and equal opportunity.

Despite the forces of resistance and constraint, we found that the brightest leaders could and would still find ways to accentuate and preserve freedom.

### Leading to Flexibility with Vendors

The first way to maintain freedom is to discuss this issue with software and hardware vendors. Their self-interest is to root themselves deep in the organization—and in the process increase the switching costs involved of going to another vender. A leader who is aware of this can create a strategy to lower the switching costs. In the final agreement, a leader or organization that truly wants telework to work will ensure that flexibility concerns are addressed. Beware of high switching costs and make sure you have a cost-effective exit plan in case you need it down the road. As vendors push for fewer short-, mid-, and long-term alternatives, leaders should push for more alternatives. As vendors attempt to limit compatibility with other software platforms, leaders should argue for more compatibility. A stractical mind-set means not settling for arrangements that could reduce discretion down the road.

### Leading to Flexibility on the Web

Another practical way individuals and organizations can ensure their flexibility is embracing software on the Web. Salesforce.com has built an entire business model on Web-based applications, software, and platforms that can be changed, modified, enhanced, or discarded as firms change and grow. What underpins this business model is the notion of flexibility. Instead of trying to embed a technology, particularly software, into the hardware of an organization (and, by so doing, reduce future choices), Salesforce.com markets choices, flexibility, and alternatives. This isn't a Salesforce.com endorsement. Indeed, other companies such as Facebook and entire communities have turned to open-source software not because it's free, even though at first blush that's what seems so valuable, but because it adds a great deal of flexibility to their operations.

*Stractical minds don't trade flexibility for technology. Just the opposite—making telework work means using technology to enhance flexibility.*

## USING SWOT ANALYSIS FOR TELEWORK

There isn't an MBA program in our country (or other countries for that matter) that doesn't teach the SWOT analysis planning tool to help craft organizational strategy. The tool is so commonplace many leading business schools are declaring it passé. We just like it because of its simplicity. And we feel that it can help stractical leaders decide how and under what conditions to make telework work.

A decision about integrating telework technology or telework arrangements into the organization must meet at least one of the criteria—that is, it must address the "S," the "W," the "O," or the "T." If leaders find that a telework decision can't address at least one of these magic letters, they should not move the organization to telework—or they should at least wait until conditions or technology changes before moving forward.

## Strengths

The "S" stands for strengths. Telework addresses the "S" when it makes the individual or organization stronger in an already strong core area. Said differently, these telework arrangements play into strengths. The strong get stronger when telework works. One small consulting company we know encouraged remote working and recruited home-based workers across the country to reduce its operating costs and increase responsiveness to its clients. The staff consultants were already used to working autonomously and traveled frequently to client sites. However, by dispersing the workforce the company was able to divide client sites into regions covered by local teams. Not only did the company reduce expenses associated with maintaining a centralized office, it allowed consultants to be on-site quicker when needed. This is a simple example of how telework satisfies the "S" part of the analysis. The firm's strengths of rapid response to its clients got stronger because it made telework work.

## Weaknesses

Even if a telework arrangement doesn't make a person or organization stronger, it could reduce the "W" factor. The "W" is about deploying telework arrangements to neutralize weaknesses. This is important since weaknesses, if left unchecked, ruin both people and organizations. We know of a consulting company that turned to telework to stem a weakness that was threatening its very survival. This consulting concern was based out of the Greater New York City metro area and provided specialty consulting services to large municipal and state crime labs throughout the world. These services aimed at improving the preservation of evidence and reinforcing the chain of custody for the flow of evidence from the crime scene through the lab into the courts. Further specialized consulting services on how to speed DNA testing were also offered. This firm counted on numerous clients throughout the world. But its clients couldn't always count on them. Much of the consulting required on-site evaluation, as each crime lab has its own unique physical setup. But delays, traffic, and just generally poor infrastructure meant that consultants couldn't easily get out of New York's notoriously difficult JFK and LaGuardia airports. The company's reliability was in jeopardy as a result of airport problems in the Greater NYC metro area.

Realizing that this weakness was becoming a fatal flaw, the firm hired independent contractors based in hub cities such as Atlanta, Baltimore, and Charlotte. These contractors, many of whom were retired police officers or investigators, went through on-site training up in New York. After their initial training, they received files, information, and database and server access. When a client requested an on-site visit, the company could dispatch contractors who would not run into airport problems. Client satisfaction greatly improved as the company could be counted on to deliver the right person at the right time, without delays or cancellations, to the specific crime lab.

## Opportunities and Threats

A "T" (threat) often leads to an "O" (opportunity)—that's why we discuss the two factors together. As an example, one can examine how Microsoft uses blogs not only to provide technical information and tips to customers but also to gather customer input, find bugs in applications, and learn of competitor products. Customer comments left in the blogs can be very candid and expose potential problems with the company's products. Although many companies might be leery of airing dirty laundry across the Web, Microsoft turns this risk into advantage by drawing on customers as a source of new ideas and solutions for problems. The company even goes so far as to provide MVP (most valued professional) awards to those customers that provide the most insightful experiences or information.

## DECIDING WHAT TO INVEST IN

A leader's decision regarding the purchase of technology to make telework work should never be a captive of circumstance or a random act of technological ignorance. Instead, it should provide stractical value. And stractical value is realized when the leader makes a new telework arrangement address a strength, weakness, opportunity, or threat.

Before committing to a telework arrangement, make sure its use will do at least one of the following:

- Enhance a current strength.

- Neutralize a weakness.

- Seize a fleeting opportunity.

- Counter a competitive threat.

Two key variables are essential in developing and refining the stractical mind-set. Remember, making telework work is less about technology and more about changing a mind-set: Value and Cost ("V" and "C"). Along with the SWOT analysis, examining the "V" and the "C" propositions will help craft mental models that are stractical in nature.

The "V" stands for the value proposition. We're not sure who owns this concept, but we do know that it's applicable to helping leaders make telework work and tends to fall a bit more along the strategy side of the stractical equation. The nexus behind the value proposition is that a given process, resource, program, or policy should create value for the individual, team, or organization. When you're contemplating a telework investment, one of the first questions to ask and answer is, How is this telework arrangement going to add value? The question is elegant in its simplicity. Leaders and

*How do we know if telework works? We know when the new arrangement either adds value or reduces costs. It really works when it does both!*

organizations that made telework work invariably asked this very question. Those that couldn't make it work seemed to have glossed over this critical query.

In contrast to the value proposition is the "C" or cost containment proposition. Typically, leaders and organizations want to reduce their living or operating costs. Ideally, telework should help drive down costs.

This discussion illustrates a key point—one that is among the most elemental in business success. The formula goes something like this:

$$\text{Profit} = \text{Value} - \text{Costs}$$

This should be easy to digest as it applies to leading telework. Technology's influence on work should either create or add value or reduce operating and transaction costs. Ideally, it should do both.

---

### BUILDING BENEFIT

We consulted with a nonprofit group where solving these equations via telework surfaced. The issue involved governance and the Board of Directors. The directors were all volunteers who didn't get paid for their service of advising, mentoring, monitoring, and evaluating the staff of this nonprofit group. Making the directors' job more difficult was the complex pseudo-governmental mission that this organization attempted to fulfill—housing and medical outreach to people who lived below the poverty line. Poverty, affordable housing, access to health care, and job retraining are complex policy issues that require investments of time and thought.

The directors were feeling overwhelmed. They'd show up for a meeting and have balance sheets, income statements, and stractical documents thrown their way. They felt unprepared. A director who missed one meeting would be left in the dark, playing catch-up for the next meeting and probably beyond it.

We suggested integrating technology with the work of governance. We began by asking, How can technology allow directors to perform their duties better? Then we asked how technology could allow directors to be more efficient in performing their duties.

Several applicable takeaways were implemented. The most notable was creating a "Director's Dashboard" section on this nonprofit's

Web site. Any director could log on from any location and review meeting minutes, vote on important issues, and view upcoming agendas.

Balance sheets and bylaws were archived on this Web site for easy access. The Web site also had a blog and Instant Messenger function where a director could raise an issue such as fundraising for the food pantry and get some real-time feedback.

Almost immediately, the organization saw an increase in the quality of governance. Directors came to their meetings more informed, and as a result they asked better questions. Missing a meeting was no longer a death knell for a director; technology allowed catch-up speed that would otherwise have been impossible. This new telework arrangement didn't turn lazy directors into hard workers. It did, however, create a context that made it easier for those who wanted to contribute to do so.

The nonprofit case really harks back to the equation given earlier. When leaders think stractically, telework either enhances value or reduces costs—or it does both.

## TIMING IS CRITICAL

We've discussed the importance for stractical leaders to evaluate the short- and long-term benefits and challenges to their telework investments. Essentially, this answers the questions *why* and *what*. However, it is equally important to understand *when* to implement. It is unclear why so few leaders wrestle with the *when* question—when to try to make telework work—since it is such a critical factor. The fact is that most technology purchases are impulse purchases. This is hard to believe since the ramifications of such purchases last months, even years. Don't feel alone here; we also fall into this camp. Let's look at an example to illustrate why the *when* question is so important.

**IMPULSE PURCHASE**

A good friend bought a new cell phone while walking around the mall. Forget about the complete lack of research that went into this hardware and network plan purchase. The real problem in the impulse purchase was that our friend didn't set aside time to learn about his new phone. The lady at the mall desk showed him the absolute basics: how to make and receive calls and how to enter contacts. When he got home, he had other family and work issues to attend to, and the owner's manual got shuffled away to a dark, damp place. Three months later, he still knew how to perform only those three functions out of the hundred-plus different functions the instrument offered him.

The cell phone case highlights a common theme that surrounds technology purchases that are also impulse purchases—people forget or are unable to find time to learn about the technology. The corollary here is equally true, though. Those who plan technology purchases are more likely to set aside time to learn about the technology.

If you think this story doesn't apply to the corporate world, think again. The more leaders we spoke with, the more stories we heard about what happened when organizations became enamored of a new technology. They rushed to purchase software or hardware, paying little attention to adopting the new technology or training the people who would have to use it.

A related finding from our observations is the tightness of the time window in which people will actually learn about a newly purchased or adopted technology. Generally, we've found that the twenty-four-hour period after the purchase is of critical importance. What this means is that for telework to work, the incubation time (time spent reading the manual, testing, and playing with the technology) is of critical importance and the time frame is short. Very few people can even find their owner's manual thirty days after getting the new technology, let alone read it to enhance their performance.

*Make sure you allow ample time to learn and experiment immediately after the purchase of a new technology.*

The key lesson here is that when you purchase a technology, the *when* of it is critical. For even the simplest technology supporting telework, leaders need to make sure that users have time after the purchase to learn. Deploying technology across a business unit or company requires that stractical leaders incorporate change management, training, and learning time into the overall plan.

## FINISH SECOND . . . AND WIN BIG!

Another key issue for stractical leaders in deciding when to adopt technology is that of being first or second. It does not necessarily pay to be first. A first-mover strategy requires considerable patience and willingness to experiment, as well as massive up-front investments of time and money.

### LEARN FROM FIRST MOVERS

Our friend, the restaurateur, started the second—not the first—Asian fusion eatery in his city. Although the first restaurant created some initial brand recognition and enjoyed an early monopoly on the Asian fusion crowd, the two restaurants were soon moving in different directions. Our friend's clientele was expanding along with his margins. The same could not be said for the other restaurant.

We were curious at the differences between the two. "How do you explain this?" we asked our friend.

"Easy," he said, "I was second."

We didn't understand. "Yeah, in America, second means you lost. He should be winning, but he isn't."

He barely looked up from his drink. "You don't get it. I'm glad I was second. You see, being first means he took all the risks. He experimented. He was the guinea pig. But you never want to experiment too much with your customers. So I just sat back and learned from him. Learned what to do and learned what not to do. He spent all the money on the marketing survey. He did his R&D. I just watched what he did and made a deal with myself to follow what he was doing right

> **LEARN FROM FIRST MOVERS cont.**
>
> and capitalize on where he was missing the mark. A simple case in point was his hours. He wasn't open Sunday at 11:00. The church crowd is out and they're looking for a good place to eat and many of them want something different from Applebee's. He could've filled that need, but for some reason he didn't. But I did. My costs and risks were so much lower than his. I just watched. Yeah, given the choice between being a first mover or a strong second mover, I'll choose a strong second mover every day of the week. That's where true advantage lies. In second. Not being first."

This strong second mover principle enjoys applicability way beyond the food service industry. As we talked to leaders and studied technology successes and failures, we found the strong second mover concept particularly relevant to telework arrangements.

One group that we talked to reminisced about a knowledge management software aimed at fixing defects and enhancing the cross-talk between the engineering and manufacturing groups. This software was supposed to help identify defects and allow a forum and knowledge repository between engineers and production people to help address the defect. Unfortunately, access to this software was uneven and seemed haphazard. While the engineering group possessed the requisite hardware and software, the manufacturing group did not. The knowledge management software was left largely unused. When asked to reflect on this failure, managers and production people alike agreed it was because they were the vendor's first customer within their particular industry. Because of that, they had just too many bugs to deal with—too many trials by fire and too much learning by doing for the software to gain any traction. They had nobody to learn from but themselves, because they were pioneers in a territory that nobody else had traveled.

*Learn from the successes and failures of first movers to become a strong second mover. Chances are, it will be less risky and costly than going it alone as a first mover.*

Again, the key lesson here is for leaders to know when to implement new technology. We suggest employing a strong second mover approach. More often than not, this telework strategy will lessen both costs and risk. To really gain the full benefits of a second mover strategy, commit to learn the upsides and downsides of telework arrangements from first movers. Leaders can also do this by networking and asking questions. Benchmark other companies to learn from their successes and failures. Attending conferences and reading trade journals are effective ways to learn as much as possible about a new technology before investing too much in its deployment. For a strong second mover advantage to work, leaders and organizations must become sensitive to what is being done around them. It is this TI or technological intelligence that will make or break the strong second mover strategy for both the leader and the organization.

*To truly reap the benefits of strong second movers, a learning mentality is required.*

## NO TIME TO RESIST

Finally, a stractical mind-set is needed to frame the timing and the *when* question in its appropriate context. It is the intersection of leadership and stractical thinking that is important here.

---

**GOING ALONG OR DIGGING IN**

Building off our earlier discussion in Chapter 1 regarding technology in a distribution facility In the late 1990s, we learned of two distribution centers that were experimenting with bar code reading guns to replace the old paper-sticker labeling system. Wal-Mart had been using bar code readers in its distribution system for years, and this company felt that it needed to embrace the technology to keep up.

In one distribution center, the general manager of the center announced to the 1,200-person organization that they were going to move toward bar code readers. He made this announcement thirteen months before the actual adoption.

**GOING ALONG OR DIGGING IN cont.**

In the other distribution center, the general manager announced the same news in the same way—but did so three weeks before the actual adoption. Which do you think worked better?

It may seem counterintuitive, but the three-week notice worked monumentally better. In general, the manager saw less resistance, smoother adoption, and less regression tendencies toward the old system. Thirteen months simply proved too long. It gave certain core constituencies resistant to the idea the time to organize and launch an offensive about the new arrangement. It also gave too much time for imagination to kick in and for people to dream up illogical and unreasonable scenarios. A couple of people suggested that robots were next and that they'd all be replaced.

In contrast, three weeks caught people off guard. The shorter horizon prevented resistance from mobilizing and organizing. At this point, the train was right in front of people and they had no time to think of alternatives.

There's no quick and easy answer here, but we can see how technology and leadership come together in cases such as this. Both distribution centers had similar cultures. One manager was aware of the resistance to change in general and technology in particular. This made all the difference, as the *when* question was of paramount importance. The other distribution center leader lacked this awareness, and the entire organization suffered as a result.

*There's a time and place to announce and implement telework; never take this decision lightly.*

## PLAN WELL *AND* FIX FAST

As telework arrangements become more complex, even the best leaders or technologists will be unable to predict some aspects of technol-

**LEARNING ON THE FLY**

One of our restaurateur friend's more telling contrarian perspectives was on strategy implementation.

Sitting in his restaurant after it had closed one evening, our friend took a long, slow sip of wine. "We had some problems tonight," he said.

"You don't sound overly concerned," we offered back.

"No. That's what made it a great night for the restaurant."

Now we put down our drinks. "What are you talking about now?"

"C'mon, guys. Tonight we were trying out a new menu. This was a strategic direction. A strategic change. We added more fresh fish to our menu. We thought we did our due diligence. We practiced the new dishes. Ate them ourselves. Pilot-tested them on friends and family with rave reviews. But at some point, strategy ends, execution begins, service is emphasized, and learning starts. And that's what happened tonight."

ogy. It becomes virtually impossible to anticipate and fix every single problem of interface or compatibility. To plan well and fix fast, stractical leaders first recognize that problems will surface. The leaders and implementers are expecting the difficulties, are ready for them, and will demonstrate exemplary service by fixing them quickly. The plan-and-fix approach also illustrates the point where the leader recognizes when strategy becomes tactical.

The plan-well-and-fix-fast approach is gaining popularity in the IT world. A recent and illustrative example is a large university we know that attempted to launch new enterprise resource planning software. Planning, concepts, and strategic discussions are clean and sterile, but the implementation of ERP software is anything but—the software tries to integrate so many disparate functions. In the case of this school, the new ERP system would cobble together such diverse functions as admissions, class registration, payroll and finance, and HR.

**BRINGING IN ERP**

Going in, the university leaders knew there would be problems. They had beta-tested and pilot-tested the new software, but realized that they still had too many unexplained variables that could not be detected in the planning and screening stages. They reasoned courageously that the best way to move forward was to implement the software, communicate expectations, and be ready to fix and address any bugs that surfaced. Essentially, they rolled out a major software program that was not completely understood or evaluated. Keep in mind that this was a strategic decision, and that they felt they had learned as much as they could in beta and pilot testing.

The results were mixed with a lean toward favorable. The launch of this type of ERP software has caused severe financial pain to some of the world's most sophisticated industry giants—Nike, Hershey, and even Hewlett-Packard. Compared to these firms, the university got a passing grade. The ERP software was launched on schedule and under budget. However, it generated several payroll mistakes that were fixed with a quick-strike service team as the problems surfaced.

The school followed the lead of our friend the restaurateur. Together, these examples can offer a countervailing perspective on how to tactically implement complex ideas such as telework arrangements. Rather than naively thinking that all bugs can be worked out, that planning and implementation would run smoothly, and that they knew all the answers beforehand, they believed otherwise on each and every point.

Maybe just as important, and as our friend suggested, a deeper, more sophisticated learning occurs during execution. As long as an individual or organization is willing and able to learn and learn quickly, this type of knowledge capture is tough to beat. Our follow-up conversation with him reflects exactly this sentiment:

"You back on track?" we asked.

"Didn't skip a beat. We learned more on that Friday night on what our customer fish preferences were, how to prepare our different types of fish, and what wine selection and sides should be offered alongside our fish. No amount of pilot testing or Internet research could've helped me here. I had to learn by doing. And we did. By the way, that night, we had what military guys call an After Action Review. And it helped enormously."

An After Action Review (AAR) is a military procedure designed to capture learning and lessons right after a training session. During a typical thirty-minute review, the platoon or company discusses what went right and should continue. They also ask what went wrong and how those errors should be fixed, negated, or addressed. It is a postmortem review done almost immediately after an activity or even while implementing it. A stractical mind-set probably prefers AARs as much as possible. We think they are important, if not essential, when a leader or organization adopts the launch-then-fix approach to telework as opposed to the fix-then-launch approach.

## SUMMING UP STRACTICAL LEADERSHIP AND DECISION MAKING

Identifying the tactics to carry out a successful telework strategy is not easy. It requires a leader to balance several seemingly disparate concepts. Throughout this chapter we have illustrated the need for leaders to understand not only why they should implement technology to transform their organization but also when they should implement it in the face of the strategic challenges they are likely to face. The final concept is to identify the granular details to put everything in motion. Telework requires both strategy and execution. Think stractically!

*Implementation and execution may seem like tactical decisions, but stractical thinking shows otherwise. More often than not, execution is equal parts tactical and strategic.*

# GUIDING PRINCIPLES

Strategy without execution may result in many well-meant ideas that never get off the ground. Likewise, tactical execution with no overriding strategy may resemble a flurry of disjointed activities. Neither can ultimately get the organization to its goal of leveraging technology to perform better. Successful telework arrangements are the result of leaders who develop the right strategy and implement the tactics to carry out the plan. Keep in mind the following guiding principles:

*Develop a stractical mind-set.* Envision the short-term and long-term implications as they apply to technology. Balance the potential impact with an understanding of the challenges that will undoubtedly accompany deploying and executing the technology.

*Remember that technology means interdependence.* Understand how technology is woven through the organization—the connections between personal and professional functions. Introducing new technology to create telework requires an understanding of how work, processes, policies, and tools and work functions will change.

*Keep the SWOT mind-set.* Creating a telework arrangement should address a strength, weakness, opportunity, or threat. Incorporating new technology should build on a core strength, neutralize a weakness, mitigate an external threat, or create new opportunities.

*Keep VC in mind as well.* A telework investment must create value for the individual and the organization. Understand (and quantify) the positive impacts to the individual, team, or organization. Also understand how the technology will help drive down costs, whether the hard costs of infrastructure or the soft costs of productivity and risk avoidance.

*Maintain flexibility—don't be constrained by technology.* Remember that technology and telework should not constrain the individual or organization. Integrating technology into work arrangements should always enhance personal or organizational flexibility.

*Pay attention to timing.* Introducing new technology or work arrangements involves communication, change management, adoption, and learning. Incorporate these factors into the deployment plan and decide when to communicate the change, as well as building in time to accommodate the organization's learning curve.

*Second movers can finish first.* Mitigate some of the costs and risks of telework by learning how other organizations are employing technology in their business. Network, benchmark, attend conferences, read trade journals, and do whatever possible to learn as much as possible about a new technology before investing too much in its deployment.

*Expect the unexpected.* Leaders will never be able to predict all the issues or problems that will arise with telework. When deploying new technology the organization needs to be cognizant of this gap and be prepared to move quickly to address and face challenges that emerge. Remember, plan well and fix fast.

# 3

# HOW LEADERS CREATE THE ORGANIZATIONAL DNA THAT MAKES TELEWORK SUCCESSFUL

*I start with the premise that the function of leadership is to produce more leaders, not more followers.*

**Ralph Nader**

Who knows you best? Your spouse? Father? Mother? Best friend? Probably, none of the above. This may be tough for some to confront, but the one with the best knowledge isn't even a "who"; it is or will soon be an "it"—a computer. With the advent of super-fast micro-processors, it is now possible to map a large portion of the human genome, essentially the DNA sequence and puzzle that makes us who we are. Without technology and computers, this task would be impos-sible to undertake. It may seem like technology is getting the upper hand on humanity. We think otherwise. Technology needs people, too. And we found that in cases of teleworking success, the human element of leadership and management always trumped and drove technology, not vice versa. The true essence of teleworking leaders is that they make technology work for them; they rarely if ever become slaves of technology.

There is an adage that says not all HR managers are leaders, but all leaders are HR managers. As it applies to teleworking, we couldn't agree more. Throughout this chapter we will cover some general but essen-tial human resource practices that any leader can employ to make sure that the human element drives teleworking—not the other way around. Because that makes all the difference in the world in making telework work.

## UNDERSTANDING THE JOB

Henry David Thoreau has many famous quotes, but none is more apropos to our topic than "For every thousand hacking at the leaves of evil, there is one striking at the root." And the concept applies throughout human life, not just to questions of good and evil. The root of all management of people is the job. Without a real and authentic understanding of what the job is, no one can do a good job of recruiting people, selecting people, training them, evaluating them, or paying them. The very best teleworking leaders seem to inherently understand the criticality of this point. Not all jobs are good candidates for teleworking arrangements, and a careful job analysis is required before a leader can build, train, and evaluate a high-performing teleworking team.

*Not all jobs are suitable for teleworking arrangements. Leaders must analyze and determine which jobs are and which jobs are not.*

## ANALYZING THE JOB

A core leader responsibility is then to determine which jobs are suitable for teleworking and which ones are not. While there is no hard-and-fast rule here, we can offer some guiding leadership principles to help the teleworking leader make that decision.

Before we plow into our principles, keep in mind these facts. More and more jobs can be teleworked. We further bet that at least a small percentage of any job can be teleworked. Determining that percentage is an important leadership responsibility.

### The Need for Contact

Rule number one in our job analysis involves the *law of contact*—the greater the contact, both with people or things, the less likely the job can be adequately teleworked. Put differently, teleworking won't work as well when physical contact between two people or a person and a machine is a critical part of the job. Using a sports metaphor, though, we realize that few jobs are truly contact sports. Here are a couple of contact jobs, however, that may be difficult to telework. Can firefighters telework? Maybe a little. Should police detectives telework? Perhaps a little. How about an orthodontist? A quality inspector at the end of a production line? Maybe a little.

A corollary to this rule is that jobs that require more of our five senses are difficult to package into teleworking arrangements. You wouldn't want the Sam Adams beer tester teleworking, would you? No, a beer tester needs to see, smell, taste, and maybe even touch the beer. We depend upon those sensory experiences when we gulp down the lager. This is a job that cannot be easily teleworked.

*Great teleworking leaders know that multisensory jobs are tougher to transform into teleworking arrangements.*

As teleworking leaders examine the job, they must also account for two other critical forces that interact to influence the bottom line: product characteristics and customer expectations. Keeping this notion of contact and sensory engagement in mind, take a look at the critical forces of product characteristics and customer expectations at work in the following example.

### FACE TO FACE

Interior designers who work at high-end furniture stores present special challenges to the teleworking arrangement. Fine furniture is a multisensory product. It must be seen for style but felt for comfort. Fine furniture is not a commodity item and does not compete on price; it competes on style and difference. It is not a product that can easily be captured via technology. Understanding this, customers usually want to physically be there at least once before making the purchase.

Meanwhile, interior decorating is a complex job requiring intimate and trusting relationship building; truly understanding a client's style and artistic preferences is difficult and time-consuming. It also involves the understanding and communication of abstract concepts such as

> ### FACE TO FACE cont.
>
> stylistic fit, taste, and trends. Related to this point, interior decorators are masters of context. They must expertly understand how a piece on the showroom floor will fit into the house of a client with different colors and layouts. That's why the best interior decorators make house calls to understand, see, and feel the context of the house. Clearly, then, the teleworking leader cannot easily transform this job into a teleworking one. However, the best teleworking leaders are also masters of efficiency and can tweak even these difficult jobs to be more tele-like.

We know of just one case up in Butler, Pennsylvania, at a fine furniture store called Furniture Galleries. Working at Furniture Galleries is one of the most renowned interior decorators on the Eastern Seaboard. She is a master of style, trends, and fit, and clients with both regional and national seek her counsel and advice. The problem, however, was the amount of time it took once a client came to the store. A single client could take up eight hours of this decorator's time without even making a purchase. The owner of the furniture store grasped the power of even the smallest teleworking arrangements. He led this decorator to send digital pictures of the furniture along with online PDF files of recent catalogues to customers before they came to visit. In addition, the decorator asked for home pictures or JPEG files to get an understanding of the client's current style and setting (that is, French Country, traditional, clean lines and modern). The impact was profound. Rather than starting at zero, the client and the decorator started on second base. Telework reduced physical time with the client by 50 percent, which meant more sales for the decorator and the store owner.

*The percentage of each job that can be converted to telework requires that the teleworking leader examine the interplay of the job, the product, and the customer's expectations.*

Another related area where we are seeing more and more incremental teleworking adjustments resulting in big gains is with real estate sales. Many Realtors send links and pictures of homes, schools, and neighborhoods before the first physical interaction between agent and client. Homes, like fine furniture, are difficult to package into teleworking—but it happens. For example, a Navy orthodontist in Italy once bought a house in Frostburg, Maryland, sight unseen. But sight unseen is inaccurate. She saw hundreds of digital pictures before making the purchase. So the house was seen. It just wasn't felt, touched, or smelled. The question then for the teleworking leader is what portion or percentage of the job could and should be converted to a teleworking arrangement. In other words, the leader should determine how technology can best be used to support the job.

## The Necessary Level of Connection

By and large, from both a personal and professional angle, we've observed that people tend to fall into one of two camps. Our world is divided by what we see as generalists or as specialists. Put differently, in so many of life's activities, we choose to go either an inch wide and a mile deep (specialist) or a mile wide and an inch deep (generalist). Apply it to friendships. A generalist is friends with many but has fewer deep relationships. Opposite this is the specialist who has few friendships, but those are deep and meaningful ones. Our second general rule applies to the tension between generalists and specialists. Generally, the deeper, the more intense, the more nuanced and specialized the relationship or approach to knowledge and learning, the harder it is to telework—at least initially.

Very few doctoral degrees are awarded online or via telework arrangements. The reason is simple—the level and depth of learning and knowledge transfer is just too deep to transfer in a virtual manner. The same is often said regarding mentoring relationships. The level of intimacy between mentor and protégé is harder to convey and transfer virtually. We acknowledge that it can still be done, but it is just harder to do. And failure rates will tend to be higher.

However, once the relationship is anchored and secure through a physical and intimate relationship, deep long-distance interaction is possible via a virtual world. Teleworking leaders may wish to take a *crawl, walk,* and then *run* strategy here—ramping up the teleworking arrangements after the physical interaction has been cemented. The bottom line here again is that it's the teleworking leader's duty and responsibility to examine both jobs and the relationships that these jobs require to determine which ones are better candidates for teleworking than others. Specifically, telework leaders can take stock of all the current job categories that they are involved with or supervise and ask a few basic questions:

- Why couldn't these job categories be teleworking jobs right now?
- What is holding this progression back?
- Is it technology, leadership, trust issues, or the job itself?
- How can you effect change to move forward?

Telework leaders may find that most jobs can be worked from a library, home office, airport terminal, or hotel lobby now.

## THE REALITY OF THE JOB

One of our more interesting conversations regarding the people part of teleworking took place at our friend's Asian fusion restaurant. We sat down with a senior VP of employee development at a large regional accounting firm.

---

### LOOKING FORWARD

"Tomorrow's the day we move forward with our teleworking initiative," he declared proudly.

We nodded and it made sense to us. Accounting work involves little contact and demands the use of few human senses. Accountants tend to work with data as opposed to people or things. In our mind, this job category was a prime candidate for teleworking.

He put down his glass of wine. "This is going to be like taking candy from a baby."

We looked at each other. "Jack, we're not tracking here. What do you mean?"

"Oh, come on. Who wouldn't want to telework? How easy can life get? Working from home. Ultimate flexibility. Come and go as you please. We're probably offering these people a damn vacation. It's all a crock to me."

He didn't skip a beat. "Thirty years ago, I wish I had this type of deal. Easy street for me. On the beach by 10 a.m. Shoot out a couple of e-mails. Answer a few phone calls. I bet these damn teleworkers will work less than two hours a day."

At this juncture, we needed the wine. "Jack, I don't think that's exactly what teleworking is. And we hope when you recruited people into this new teleworking plan, you didn't paint it all as a walk down Easy Street. Did you?"

"You know-it-alls don't know that much about recruiting, do you? C'mon. It's a sales job, but this teleworking job is so easy, no salesmanship is really needed. Telework is like a Lexus, boys—it sells itself."

Jack's conversation and perspective revealed a complete lack of understanding of how teleworking can work and how it can't. Sadly, it illustrated that as a leader he wasn't ready for teleworking. He wasn't managing his human resources, and that became evident six months later at the same restaurant.

Eventually, we brought up the topic knowing full well where the answer would take us. "Jack, six months have passed. Are you ramping up your teleworking plans?"

Looking dejected and taking a sip of wine with his humble pie, he replied, "Nope. We're actually thinking about canning it.

"It's been one of our firm's biggest failures on so many fronts. Both logistically and trustwise. We told 'em it would be easy. That their life would be better. But that's not how it ended up. It got worse. Their lives got worse. Both professionally and personally.

"We had twenty-four people sign up for the new teleworking deal. Only four accountants are still doing it full-time. Six people out-and-out quit. Ten came back to our office, which was a pain logistically since we had converted their offices to storage areas and a server room for our computers. And four are on a hybrid schedule, twenty hours at home and twenty on-site. What a mess, too. Morale has never been lower."

"How so?" we asked.

**LOOKING FORWARD cont.**

"Well, I just don't know how to put it any other way. Our people feel lied to. We told 'em it would be peaches and cream. But it's been the pits. Instead of working less, people worked more. They were the hard chargers to begin with, and when they worked from home they couldn't turn themselves off. It was sad in some ways. From our very best accountant, we'd get e-mail at four in the morning. When he quit two weeks ago, he said during an exit interview that teleworking almost ruined his marriage. And we thought we were doing this guy a favor. The problem was that he couldn't separate work and play when he was at home."

This was starting to get depressing—and it got even worse.

"Some of it was just crazy. One guy had a huge dog at his house that was also a barker. Whenever we were on a conference call and the dog got all antsy it would bark and howl. Not the most professional thing you want to hear on a conference call. Another lady's three-year-old couldn't understand that Mommy was at work and couldn't be bothered. But you'd hear the kid crying. It was just bad."

"Is that it?" we hoped.

"Pretty much. We also saw that few people had a designated office space or the infrastructure to support teleworking. Believe it or not, we had two accountants that didn't have a speakerphone or high-speed Internet. They were still using dial-up!"

We put on our coaching hats. "So, whose fault was this?"

He thought for a bit and spoke in measured words. "This was our fault. Clearly, not all our teleworkers were ready from an infrastructure vantage. But it was the psychological that killed us here. Nope. It was us. We failed as leaders. We never put all the information up front for our employees to make informed decisions. And we're accountants, for godsake!"

This was a tough lesson for our friend Jack. But he got it in the end. This was both a leadership problem and a human resource issue. One of the best ways to increase the quality of your recruiting pool and the long-term success of employees is to present what academics call a realistic job preview, or RJP. Leaders give their future or current employees an RJP when they inform them of all aspects of the job, both desirable and undesirable. Jack fell into the trap that many aspiring leaders fall into—he only previewed what he thought were the positive aspects of the new teleworking arrangements. In the end, this was a fatal flaw as it jacked up the expectations of the people signing up for telework. When reality didn't meet expectations, the accountants were surprised and angry, and as Jack mentioned, they felt betrayed or lied to. All leaders, but particularly those who lead teleworkers, are in the business of managing expectations. And that means being realistic and truthful about what the teleworking job entails. Give RJPs that portray the benefits, drawbacks, and occasional pitfalls of teleworking. And as Ralph Nader highlights in the opening quote of this chapter, give people the information to make informed decisions and to be able to lead themselves. This is particularly important when it comes to teleworking, but we've seen time and again that both employees and managers start out with misinformed, misguided, and just flat-out wrong visions and expectations of what teleworking really entails.

*Telework is harder than many expect. Great teleworking leaders prepare their future teleworkers for this reality so they are ready to deal with it.*

## SELECTING THE PEOPLE

Once you've analyzed a job and understand whether it can be teleworked or not, you can—if you're really good—write the job formally in terms of a job specification, job requirements, and job duties. After that, you've set the stage to recruit talent by offering an RJP. Then comes the problem of selecting people for the teleworking team. The goal of selection is to find the right person for the right job at the right time. More than anything, the person needs to fit the job. And just as some jobs can't be teleworked, some people—even some of your brightest and best talent—won't fit well with a teleworking arrangement. We offer some guiding principles about what you should look for when selecting talent for the teleworking team.

Selection is so very important to both leaders and HR managers since once people join an organization, it's difficult and expensive to get them out if things don't work. A common maxim is *hire slow, fire fast*. As it applies to teleworking, we suggest staying close to the spirit of that message. Be deliberate in the hiring and selection stage, and if there's one place to add science to the leader's decision-making process, it would be in the area of selecting in those that can telework and selecting out those that can't.

*Leaders make sure the right people fit the right job at the right time.*

## Fitting Personality

As a leader, employ both formal and informal tools to gauge if someone has the right mentality, personality, and disposition to do telework. There are two ways to do this. The first is scientific and is common for large companies and organizations like Target, Microsoft, the FBI, and the CIA: Give a personality test. That's the science. Now the gut: Observe and interview. The great thing about personality is that it hardly ever changes, and when it does, it does so at a snail's pace. The personality someone had at age six is remarkably similar to the personality they have now. While attitudes and certainly moods tend to change frequently, personality is heavily resistant to change. That's good for the leader. Based on our research and our experience, we've identified some personality traits to look out for both formally and informally.

*Leaders should never dismiss extroverts as teleworkers out of hand. Extroverts provide much-needed energy to the teleworking experience, which could otherwise become stale, dead, and boring.*

We disagree with the pundits and experts who contend that an organization should always assign telework to introverted employees. Teleworking some functions to introverted talent may be acceptable, but we believe that you also need extroverted people to make telework work. These are the people that can infuse their energy into electrons and protons. Introverts may feel solace and comfort not having to communicate from an off-site and out-of-mind location. But that isn't what teleworking is about. Actually, it's about communicating more—not less. Many leaders and organizations may find that they may need, believe it or not, to over-communicate early on in the teleworking process. To do that, leaders should be able to blend extroverts into their teams to jump-start the communication component of teleworking. Ideally, leaders should look for a balance of introverts and extroverts to create a healthy and successful mix.

## Trust and Responsibility

While optical fiber may be the formal architecture in which teleworking works, the social infrastructure is equally important—and it runs on trust. For leaders to build a teleworking scheme on trust requires the selection and hiring of conscientious talent. Thankfully, conscientiousness and integrity are personality traits, which means some people have more than others, and leaders can test for them both formally (via tests) and informally (background checks). Do both.

> *Trust is the grease that makes teleworking work.*

We talk more about trust later, but suffice to say trust really is the X factor in making telework work. In a typical and traditional office complex, both overt and subtle control tactics are in place to make sure people are doing what they are supposed to be doing. The simplest control mechanism of all, just watching, is powerful in a typical office but can't be done nearly as much or nearly as well in telework. So leaders must shift from a control-oriented mind-set to a commitment-oriented one. For leaders, the lesson is simple. For people to fit into teleworking jobs they shouldn't need to be controlled; they should be committed.

Leaders should also be on the lookout for only the most responsible talent to fit into teleworking arrangements. Related to this point, teleworking talent should be able to work relatively unsupervised and with little guidance as both supervision and guidance may be thousands of miles away and may take hours to track down. In any decentralized type of organization, leaders want the type of employees that Ralph Nader describes in our opening quote—those able to lead and manage themselves. In decentralized networks—and teleworking is the ultimate in decentralization—workers must have the capacity and willingness to operate

> *Teleworkers should be responsible and capable of independent thought and action.*

independently, decisively, and without much expectation of guidance and instruction.

## Communicators

As mentioned earlier, the lifeblood of teleworking is solid, accurate, and timely communication. It should come as no surprise then that leaders should place people in teleworking arrangements only if they have demonstrated adequate communication skills. When we say *communication skills,* we are talking both formal and informal and both written and verbal. A great example that brings in all elements was a case that a colleague shared with us. The story goes something like this.

### COMMUNICATION RULES

One large retail giant allowed one of its employees to telework half the week in a marketing and promotion capacity. The leader in charge, though, failed to adequately assess fit. While unobserved, this employee would visit pornographic Web sites, and one of these sites loaded a virus onto the company laptop. When he e-mailed his colleagues, he was unintentionally spreading that virus. In addition, this employee would send and forward inappropriate jokes from his off-site location, again on the firm's laptop. Adding insult to injury, the employee could not write well and his e-mails were often confusing, inappropriate, and written in shorthand—signing off on one e-mail "LOL and LUV U BG TME!"

Here we have an employee that shouldn't be working off-site. (Perhaps this one shouldn't have been on-site, for that matter!) But some people do work better in a controlled, highly supervised environment like an office complex, and he was one of them. When he wasn't in that environment, he wasted his and the firm's time, engaged in inappropriate behavior that could ultimately have harmed the business, wasn't a bit responsible, and lacked the general communication skills to do well as a teleworker. This may seem like it's all his fault, but we place the fault on the leader in not fitting the person with the job. The teleworking leader is truly a matchmaker.

## Testing and Piloting

Leaders can take a page out of the HR playbook by sampling before buying. More and more companies are employing work sample tests to select and fit people for hiring, promotion, or transfers. The concept is rooted in solid logic. Before filling a position, the leader should have some comfort that the person can do the job and should at least demonstrate some proficiency before the decision is made. Believe it or not, this concept, while simple, is only now starting to catch on. There was a time when universities would hire a professor only by interview—without knowing anything about the prospect's teaching skills. Now many universities require that applicants teach a live class prior to receiving an offer.

Telework leaders can apply the same dominant logic. Before fitting anyone into a telework assignment, have them do a work sample test. It needn't be sophisticated or complex. And for teleworking, the work sample begins with e-mail correspondence. Check e-mail for professionalism, grammar, and attention to detail. This notion of attention to detail may be particularly

*Assess talent and fit by asking employees to sample telework before signing up for it.*

important for teleworkers since they have no administrative or executive assistants to proof their work before it goes out. Another attractive possibility is to ask the person to conduct an online meeting or do a Web presentation. One last tool to make sure the employee will fit into telework is to conduct a phone interview. In many respects, conducting a phone interview with a potential teleworker may be more important than a face to face interview. Reduced to its most elemental form, teleworking is about communicating over computer and phone networks. Potential teleworkers should have a baseline proficiency in both.

One of the more progressive ways to allow both leaders and employees to test-drive telework is to set up a pilot study in the physical office before rolling out the real thing. We know of one company that did just that. Most of the managers and employees on-site thought that teleworking would be a cakewalk—until, that is, they tried to do it from inside their office complex. For ninety-six hours, the whole group pretended to be a complete teleworking organization. People conference called, communicated via e-mail, instant messaged each other, and posted notes on shared folders and blogs. The only rule was that there could be no physical contact, but the job and the work still had to get done. At the end of those ninety-six hours, a core group knew they could do telework and wanted to do it. Equally, another group realized that teleworking was not for them and they probably wouldn't be too good at it. From a leader's vantage point, this scenario spells F-I-T as you have some people self-selecting *in* and some people self-selecting *out*. None of this would be possible, though, if the leadership and management within the company didn't do a pilot test first. There is no better way to give a RJP than to allow people to taste before signing up.

*Teleworking on a pilot or sample basis is good for the employee and the leader. It improves decision-making and ultimately fit as well.*

## Transparency and Fairness

We would be remiss if we didn't mention these last concerns, transparency and fairness, in making the recruiting and selection decision. In all hiring and promotion and reassignment decisions, the most important principles, above all else, are merit, fairness, and transparency. Once an organization or leadership team decides on the selection process for becoming a teleworker, it should clearly communicate this selection process to everyone concerned. Moreover, the leadership team should clearly spell out what the criteria for it are. And, of course, these criteria should be job related. If hiring criteria, including interview questions, aren't job related, the potential for lawsuits increases.

The rationale here is simple and straightforward. And it involves leadership and perception. Employees need to see the process and criteria as fair, balanced, merit-based, and transparent. If they perceive otherwise, feelings of favoritism, cronyism, or just general unfairness could kick in and damage the working environment. No work (and especially no telework) gets done when these feelings float around in an organization.

*The integrity of the selection process is critical. Communicate openly and directly regarding the process and criteria necessary to become a teleworker.*

## PROVIDE TRAINING TO BRING TELEWORKERS TO THE NEXT LEVEL

Teleworking leaders are also teleworking trainers. If you've made it this far, you are in great shape and any investment in training will be returned many times over. The reason is simple. Following our leadership and human resource management principles, the job is well understood, the recruiting of a talented pool was a success, and selection was done to ensure that the right people fit the right job at the right time. Because those functions were done well, the teleworkers at this stage are both willing and able. The leader's role is to provide basic and advanced training to take them to the next level. This involves following some basic training principles and taking some specific action steps to make telework work.

---

**THE BASICS**

Joe was a good friend of ours who teleworked as a civilian contractor for the U.S. Coast Guard. Over a cup of coffee, Joe shared some insight into his teleworking experience.

One of his most memorable lines will stick with us for a while: "I like Swiss Army knives!"

"What'd you just say?"

"I like Swiss Army knives. The old ones. The old-school ones. Not the fancy ones."

We looked at each other and wondered what was really in Joe's coffee. Then we started to see his point.

"We're all a bunch of pioneers in a way. Comparably, very few telework. It'll become mainstream someday. But it isn't there yet. And all pioneers need the basic Swiss Army knife to survive. You know, the spoon, the fork, the knife. That's all I really needed to get going. But so many organizations don't even give their people a Swiss Army knife before they pioneer into the teleworking frontier."

The metaphor made sense to us. Our experience and research tells us that the Swiss Army knife for teleworkers is training that focuses on time management and technical skills. Communication and soft skill training is important, but we'll touch on that later. Know that if leaders fail to provide this core training, teleworkers cannot eat; they will not survive. They don't have their Swiss Army knife.

*The Swiss Army knife of teleworking is training. The fork and the knife of the Swiss Army knife are time management and technical skill training.*

## Provide Structure

"I was slowly losing my life" is a common refrain of many teleworkers. Before getting prescriptive on how to fix this, great leaders should want to know *why* it occurs.

The answer is structure. A traditional corporate and office job provides structure. There's a start time; there's a stop time. And before people know it, a routine forms. The routine provides some comfort, boring as it might be. To make it to the office and back requires an alarm clock, breakfast, a commute, a lunch break, a coffee break, a commute home, and dinner. The predictability of it all provides structure. To a large extent, that all disappears with telework—and this is a serious threat to making telework work. It's gotten to the point where we've heard pundits say that teleworkers should put on professional dress, drive around the block, and return home to begin the teleworking day to develop a semblance of a routine. We're not sure about that. But we are sure that leaders must help teleworkers find their own comfort with structure and time management.

*Traditional work provides a schedule and a routine. Many teleworkers have difficulty making the transition to a schedule and routine of their own.*

Not only are teleworking leaders functioning as trainers, they are also healers, physicians. Teleworking leaders need to be on the lookout for symptoms of poor time management. Leaders can do this by monitoring progress on a project or program. When timelines start getting pushed back or the work appears sloppy, forced, and hurried, the leader should act on these symptoms to help the teleworkers develop their own personal time management programs.

The leader's formula to help the teleworker is well chronicled in many management books. At the most elemental level, time management is about the following:

- Clearly identifying the tasks that need to be done.

- Assigning a priority to each task.

- Given that priority level, scheduling the task.

- Monitoring and assessing the progress through social reminders from people (that is, boss or peer) or from technology (such as Microsoft Outlook).

- Updating and reprioritizing tasks on an as-needed basis.

We've found that among the biggest barriers to time management, task completion, and just general mental health are e-mail and instant messaging. Both are critically important, but often reverse the roles that cement the beginning of this chapter. Many teleworkers become managed by e-mail and IMs rather than have themselves managing the software. We are hesitant to say one size fits all, and there's no doubt this isn't a universal problem for teleworkers, but slavery to e-mail and IMs affects a great many people—traditional employees as well as teleworkers. The problem for teleworkers is that e-mail and IMs are the lifeblood of their existence. The trick is to use these communication tools to advance beyond survival and to keep them from becoming the bane of a teleworker's existence.

*Great leaders coach their employees to develop their own time management skills. Managing e-mail is a key factor in making telework work.*

E-mail and IMs are dangerous on two fronts. If you try to answer every e-mail as it pops up, you can never concentrate on more important tasks. E-mail is like kerosene poured on the fire of attention deficit disorder. If you answered every phone call that occurred during dinner, you couldn't eat or eat well or eat as a family. There's a time and place to answer e-mail. Leaders need to help teleworkers answer that question and assist them in devising their own strategies.

**E-MAIL MANAGER**

Listen in to one of the conversations we had with a research faculty member at a major public university—a teleworker who does a great portion of his research and writing from home.

"I can pinpoint exactly when my academic fortunes began to change," he remarked.

"When?" we asked.

"Easy. When I changed my e-mail strategy."

Interested, we pressed. "Go on."

"I used to check my e-mail throughout the day. Whenever I heard that sound, I stopped what I was doing and I read and often answered the e-mail. The problem is I couldn't ever get the time going, the momentum going to think clearly and do good research and writing. I saw every e-mail as urgent and important. And what I realized is that 99.99 percent of the e-mails are neither. So, what I do now is read my e-mail three times a day."

"Is that it?" we asked.

"Well, almost. Those three times aren't equal. The first forty-five minutes of my day I program to reading and responding to e-mails from students, faculty, and research colleagues that I've developed friendships with, both personal and work-related, throughout the world. Right before lunch, I take fifteen minutes and scan my e-mails for ones that may be truly urgent and important. Finally, the last forty-five minutes of my day I spend reading and responding to e-mails. And if I get done earlier, I play earlier. But it's really changed my life. I am so much more productive now. Those e-mail interruptions were really an excuse I used not to do any substantive work."

The dialogue with the professor highlights an important point regarding time management. Leaders must help teleworkers understand the difference between urgent and important and unimportant. The most effective teleworkers are coached to respond to the urgent and then to focus on the important priorities. Regardless of the specific time management tactics used, telework leaders need to coach and mentor their teleworkers to prioritize and schedule tasks in a way that fits their own individual working style. Some trial and error may be involved here, but for teleworkers to lead themselves they must know how to manage their time.

## Basic Technical Skills

Many people can work independently but still cooperatively. These people tend to be great candidates for telework. We often see that the only factor holding someone back is basic and core technical skills. Simply, many people want to telework but lack the confidence in their own technical skills to volunteer. This is where teleworking leadership comes into play.

Leaders can foster and improve self-confidence by providing the Swiss Army knife to teleworkers in the form of core technical skills training. This foundational training may be particularly important since no on-site IT guy is there to immediately help the teleworker.

The first step in training is to conduct a needs assessment. Never assume that the employee has all the skills to do the job. Check. With teleworking, the leader should find out if the teleworker can do the following:

- Set up a computer.

- Install software on the computer.

- Set up and install a wireless network for a home office.

- Establish e-mail accounts.

- Understand core security issues as they apply to a wireless network and file downloads.

- Initiate or dial in to join a conference call.

- Manage and file different documents.

- Use and understand basic spreadsheet functions.

- Understand how to set up distribution lists and schedule activities on an e-mail program such as Microsoft Outlook.

- Set up a BlackBerry or mobile e-mail account.

- Do basic troubleshooting.

Depending on the results of this assessment, the leader should provide training to close the gaps and build baseline proficiency on these technical skill sets. Depending on whether the teleworker is a visual, auditory, or tactile learner, the leader may wish to provide differing training formats for the individual.

*Assess whether current or future teleworkers have the core technical skills to do their job. If they don't, fix it through a variety of training options.*

The moral of the story here is that leaders don't ever need, want, or desire teleworkers to be part of the Geek Squad. What they should strive for, however, is a baseline technical proficiency so individuals at least feel comfortable and reasonably confident in teleworking.

## Leader as Decorator

In the course of our research and interviews, we came across a large regional paper company that had decided to abandon the shift to telework. Amazed that they seemed to be bucking the trend, we asked the *why* question. The answer surprised us: The chief legal counsel had recommended against teleworking based on safety, not security, concerns. This is a decidedly risk-averse stance, but the legal counsel noted that the company has little control over the chemicals, ergonomic features, and basic infrastructure (such as wiring or smoke alarms) found in the home. Conceivably, workers could work at a home that was unsafe or not compliant with Occupational Safety and Health Administration (OSHA) standards. For this legal counsel, the firm is ultimately responsible for the safety and compliance of all work areas. Since the company couldn't exert the same control or monitor people's homes or telework locations as much as it could in a traditional office setup, legal counsel thought the firm could be held liable if there were an accident at a teleworker's home. Personally, we feel that this legal advice may be just a wee bit too conservative given today's technology and business environment. We don't believe that we'd use the same legal counsel that this mill had retained, but after talking about it, there may a bit of merit to the argument—although we feel it extends way beyond liability issues. Instead, helping, advising, and coaching teleworkers to first identify and then create their tele-office is important stuff.

And to discuss this, we come full circle—back to the job. You see, the job and the office are intertwined, difficult to separate because the office—whether on-site or off-site—is where the job gets done. There's little debate that the office and the person are morphing into one. Workers are mobile, moving, wandering, and acting as offices armed with laptops, BlackBerrys, and cell phones. But even if the metamorphosis is complete, and you are a living, breathing, walking office, the principles discussed here still apply. And they apply if the office is a local library, home office, coffeehouse, or hotel lobby.

There are three guiding principles in which to coach and mentor teleworkers on their office and job: industrial engineering, ergonomics, and environment.

### Industrial Engineering

First come the principles of industrial engineering, originally made popular by Frederick Taylor. Frederick Taylor believed that jobs should be efficient, and that the layout of a work area can either help or hinder efficiency. These same rules apply for mobile offices. For teleworkers to be effective, their work area needs to be organized to get the job done. Most technologists suggest having a separate room with a separate phone line along with a separate Internet connection. Mobile or home offices that will be used for any long period of time should also have a door to reduce and filter noise and distractions. We return to the quote by Nader that opens this chapter: We want people to lead themselves. As leaders, coaches, and mentors, we don't need to tell teleworkers exactly what their office should be. We should, however, guide them and offer effective principles and best practices. Essentially, we are helping them

*Efficiency concerns still apply in the virtual world. Ensure that your teleworkers establish an efficient and effective workplace wherever that may be.*

become more effective. We've talked to hundreds of teleworkers and not a single one of them said that they were given any guidance or mentoring on how to set up their office.

### Ergonomics

The second guiding principle that telework leaders should be aware of is ergonomics. Employees often take this consideration for granted. But most companies, large and small, put some financial and cognitive resources into making their premises a comfortable and safe environment. The field of ergonomics attempts to accommodate human capabilities and limitations in the performance of a job. Ergonomics looks at such things as the work environment and the interaction of machines, furniture, and equipment with the user. This was one concern of the paper mill's management, as they felt they had no control over the safety and overall ergonomic setup of mobile offices. Empirical research makes it clear that failure to account for employee comfort and allowing poor workplace design contributes to loss of efficiency and to increased errors and waste. Leaders care about their employees, and they should care about the comfort of their teleworkers. This includes guidance about proper lighting, computer screen size and exposure, and recommended or tested chairs and furniture. This may seem like too much focus on the details—but great leaders do attend to details.

> *Leaders are responsible for both the safety and comfort of their teleworkers. Counsel and advise your teleworkers on the ergonomic considerations of the job.*

### Environment

Finally, and we mean finally, we raise the *fit* issue again. Leading and coaching means understanding what environments people excel in and offering resources or freedoms to choose those environments. For instance, many Wall Street traders and especially floor traders think and thrive in busy and noisy environments. That's where they work best. We know of a doctoral student who wrote his entire dissertation in a Starbucks. He couldn't do it in his home office or in the library; it was just too quiet there, and

> *No one size fits all when it comes to mobile offices. Help your teleworkers find the environment that best fits them and brings out their very best work.*

the quiet actually distracted him. Talk to your teleworkers. Encourage them to find an environment that suits them—with boundaries of course. The proper place to conduct a conference call is not the local Starbucks.

Leaders manage their human resources when they think about and address these small details such as work design and office choice. And it's these details that separate the merely good teleworking leaders from the great ones.

# GUIDING PRINCIPLES

Part of leading involves basic human resource principles. This applies in the traditional as well as the virtual workplace model. But telework's complexities and lack of physical interaction require an even greater embrace of the basic themes of HR. Keep in mind that almost all of these principles apply whether the teleworking candidate is currently with the organization in a traditional setup or is coming from the outside, from the open job market. Principles of job analysis, fit, recruiting and selection, training, and office design apply equally to internal and external teleworking candidates. So remember these principles while moving forward in your quest to make telework work. If you do, you'll be setting your teleworkers up for success and giving them the tools to lead themselves.

***Know the job.*** The root of all work—not just telework—is the job. Not all jobs could or should be converted into telework. It is the leader's responsibility to take a close and critical look to make that determination.

***Assess the fit.*** Just as not all jobs are suited for telework, the same is true of people. Leading is about knowing and understanding your people. This understanding is of critical importance when deciding who should telework and who should not.

# GUIDING PRINCIPLES cont.

**Set expectations.** There's nothing worse than building up expectations only to have reality pop the bubble. Many employees believe and many leaders perpetuate the myth that teleworking is easy and fun. That isn't real. That's a lie. Teleworking is real work, and it's hard work. Manage expectations and always provide a realistic job preview or RJP.

**Assess and train basic skills.** Basic skills in communication, time management, and technical issues are the Swiss Army knife for teleworkers. Without these basic, core skills they cannot survive. See and ask if they have these skills. If they don't, as a leader, you must provide them the necessary skills through training. Their success depends on it.

**Work it out.** If employees worked on-site, would leaders care about the safety, security, and comfort of their working conditions? The answer is yes—and that same care should be taken to advise, coach, and mentor teleworkers to find and build mobile offices that suit them. Whatever workspace is decided upon, it should be safe, comfortable, and efficient. These factors set the conditions for making telework work.

**4**

# LEADING TELEWORK TEAMS IN THE VIRTUAL WORLD

*Teamwork doesn't tolerate the inconvenience of distance.*
**Anonymous**

Great leadership, leadership with the implicit goal of making telework work, is indeed about teamwork. Volumes have been written about teamwork. The notion of teams itself has achieved almost iconic status in the management world. What we discovered during the course of our research was that telework teams did not contribute to telework success as much as poor telework team behaviors almost invariably led to failure. This may sound cynical, but it is a realistic and sometimes unfortunate picture painted by the leaders who experienced success and failure in the virtual world.

---

**TEAMWORK REVISITED**

Interviewing a vice president a while back, we thought we were pressing close to the limits of pessimism. The vice president was ready to throw the team out with the bathwater.

He started eloquently. "Teams . . . what a crock!"

"Be careful," we warned. "You are dancing on hallowed ground here. Teams are sacred in today's world. There's not an organization we know that doesn't value teamwork."

---

**TEAMWORK REVISITED cont.**

We were surprised at how fast he seized the opportunity, and we were even more surprised at how deeply he challenged us and turned the tables. "C'mon. Give me a break, guys. Tell me how teams work. No, tell me *really* how teams work. I know you know, but let's see if you've got the courage to swim against the huge corporate tide of team love. *Teamwork* is the most overused and abused word in all management-speak."

Strong words. We looked at each other and knew, precisely at that moment, that we were dealing with a deranged executive. One of us was about to ask for Security, but he stopped us, and what he said was compelling—and probably more accurate than what we all care to admit.

"It's all cut and paste. You know it, too. I'm convinced that our managers learn it during their MBA. This stuff about synergy and two plus two equals five is one giant organizational lie. A myth. A sad lie."

"Keep going." We started to see the strange light that he was striking.

"Especially in virtual teams or what the world calls *telework*. That's where it's the worst. What really happens on this so-called *team* is that one person does her part, another does his part, another jumps in to add her two cents, and in the end you have all of these individual contributions that are stitched together. All just cut and pasted. That's the teamwork I see every day. No real collaboration. No real deep development. Just one person's work added to an assembly line of others'. Tell me how that's a team. Tell me."

Almost in a funeral procession type of way, we got up and left. We were silent, but there was some implicit agreement felt between us. This guy was on to something. This seasoned executive may have been crazy, but that notwithstanding, he was right.

Too much of so-called teamwork is just cut and paste. Too much of what is labeled "teamwork" is nothing more than individual efforts cobbled together. That's independence—and that isn't teamwork. As described earlier, telework, and teamwork, is about interdependence.

The immediate challenge—the one staring us all in the face—is to commit to building great teams, not compilations of individuals. It is to commit to moving beyond cut and paste to something better—effective interdependence. Then and only then does the "team" moniker truly apply.

*Truly great leaders, those that make telework work, create effective interdependence—the real gauge for teamwork.*

## BALANCE THE TEAM MEMBERS

Once the somber feeling wore off, we went to work analyzing and researching. What we found does indeed hold, and it applies to all leaders—not just those leading teleworking teams *(teleteams)*. Probably less than 5 percent of all teams are worthy of the "team" label. Those that are all demonstrate effective interdependence.

Oftentimes, the best way to assess and gauge a leader is to talk to the followers. One midlevel manager that we talked to was a teleworker—not a teleleader. She'd been on the tip of the teleworking spear, working such jobs for over a decade. We asked her about her experiences in the more than fifteen virtual teams she'd been assigned to and worked for.

---

**VIRTUAL TEAM BALANCE**

"Without a doubt, the best virtual teams I've ever worked on had balance in more ways than one."

"Please describe."

"Well, virtual teams are dangerous. It's totally an outcome-related business—the teleworking world, that is. Either you deliver or you don't. Oftentimes, managers assess teleworkers on results, only reinforcing this outcome-driven environment."

We weren't following. "So?"

"Don't you see? Teleworkers are predisposed, rewarded, and coached only to get tasks done. More often than not, most virtual teams are made up of driven, task-oriented people. But a team made only of those stinks. And in the long term these teams never stick together. They just fade away."

Just as the VP earlier belted out some good points, equal kudos here as her sentiments coincided with our thoughts, theories, and evaluation of effective virtual teams that make telework work.

Effective teams are usually well balanced between task-driven and relationship-oriented people. For virtual teams, this relationship orientation is critically important, but it is often forgotten for the very reason that this seasoned teleworker brought up—teleworking is a task- and goal-oriented type of work where day-to-day processes can't be touched, felt, or seen, so leaders tend to rely on outcomes to judge and assess teleworkers. While that, in and of itself, is not a fatal flaw, not including relationship-oriented people is.

The very best teleworking leaders intuitively grasp this subtle but powerful concept. The absence of physical interaction coupled with a heavy outcome and task focus can make telework boring, stale, and dry. There's no inspiration or cohesion in these types of teams. High turnover and lower performance characterize these types of teams. That's why leaders who make telework work purposefully place relationship-oriented people on teams. These are the types who pick up the phone and call another teammate. These are the ones who Instant Message and create water cooler talk in a virtual world. These are the ones who provide the social glue for more task-oriented members, transforming the team from one of independence to one of interdependence. A team made up purely of task-oriented members creates a working atmosphere that is all work and no play. Again, especially in a virtual teamwork environment, it's the relationship builder—not the tasker—who establishes the bonds on which to build a great team. The long-term teleworker we talked with closed with a warning that all leaders of teleworkers and teleteams should heed:

*Don't succumb to the temptation to stack the virtual team with task-first people. Make sure to include some relationship-oriented members to build cohesion within the team.*

"If all team communication is done by e-mail, you've got a team of only taskers. And the leader is in trouble. And the team is staring failure in the face. On the other hand, if you've got some phone calls being made . . . where people actually pick up the phone just to talk, then the leader can breathe. There's some relationship builders on that team. And that team will be okay."

## SCREEN AND SELECT

Good leaders ask for volunteers to serve on a team. Great leaders screen and carefully select these volunteers. Think for a moment what a virtual team would be like if it had no barriers to entry. If everyone who raised a hand got a seat on the virtual team, what type of team would that look like?

---

**WIDE-OPEN TEAMS**

One leader of a virtual team answered the question about unselected team entry for us: "That's a scary team. And I've been there before. It ain't pretty."

"Go on," we prodded.

"There's no diversity on these types of teams. In my experience, at least in my organization, the people who are the first to raise a hand and volunteer for virtual teams are the techies. These are the people that like and enjoy technology. And, frankly, these are the people that aren't always the greatest in dealing with other people. I know I shouldn't say this, but the first volunteers in my organization seem to be the types that like their computer, their network, more than they like other people."

We nodded.

He continued. "While this may seem exactly like the people you want, it never really is. I failed in my first leadership job as a team leader for a virtual team for precisely this reason. The team wasn't diverse. I didn't know my people. I ended up with a homogenous virtual team that all loved technology, computers, and networks, but didn't really enjoy or know how to partner, communicate, and solve complex problems together. I learned my lesson the hard way. To make a virtual team work, you must be committed to diversity in skill sets, learning orientations, and backgrounds. Too often virtual teams are made up of the same kind of people. As leaders, we need to do better than that."

Time and again, we found that great teleworking leaders were great at the scales. They were masters of this notion of balance. When it came time for them to establish their teleworking team, they heeded much of the counsel in the preceding chapter regarding human resource management and selection—they built their team with purpose and selected members carefully. Without exception, leaders that made telework work struck a balance among personalities, skills, attitudes, and styles.

*Include all types of teleworkers within the virtual team. Be on the lookout for diverse but complementary backgrounds, communication and learning styles, and work histories.*

While this notion of diversity applies to the composition of teams, we found that diversity of communication was important, especially from the leader. It aligns closely with the task-versus-relationship discussion presented earlier. Leaders who make telework work employ both formal and informal communication styles. They mix it up. Virtual teams often suffer the fate of being too planned, too scheduled, and too coordinated. This gives an artificial feel. The great teleworking leaders mix it up with a mix of regular and formal communication with more informal and spontaneous communication.

*When leaders make teleworking work, they make it real by employing different and diverse communication patterns.*

Teleworking leaders are able to create this same type of magic. They take something that can feel, look, and smell artificial and make it real. One way they do this is through their own communication patterns. As you can tell by now, communication is a core and continuous thread in the quest to make telework work.

## CREATE A PERCEPTION OF FAIRNESS

One of the more interesting insights regarding virtual teams and making telework work arose, of all places, at a tailgate party. One of our mutual friends was talking about his three kids and, in particular, about his youngest daughter, who had just spoken her first sentence with subject, predicate, and meaning.

"It took just over two years for Emily to put three words together. But she did it, and she's got her older brother to thank."

Faking interest over our beers, we asked, "The suspense is killing us. What was it?"

"Very funny. Her brother took her ice cream and started to slop it up. She got down from her chair. Like a little lady, she put her hands on her hips and, with the attitude of her mother, screamed at the top of her lungs, 'That's not fair!'"

We all laughed—and only later did we realize that this idea of fairness is hardwired into our DNA, but is loosely configured and often improperly wired in virtual teams.

*Leaders who make telework work understand the importance of fairness and equity in building all types of teams— both virtual and traditional.*

We can't begin to tell you how much feedback we've received on this very issue of fairness and equity as it relates to making telework work. And like the experienced teleworker we quoted earlier, these comments come from the leaders' most important stakeholders—their followers.

The problem is prevalent because many leaders simultaneously lead and manage both traditional workers and teleworkers. If not handled properly, many of the traditional workers and employees feel that the teleworkers have it easy. To make matters worse, without daily physical interaction, many employees begin to assume the worst no matter how crazy the thoughts are. For instance, one teleworker said that a colleague, a traditional worker, would remark during every conference call that it must be nice to sit home and watch *Oprah* while everyone else worked. This happened on four separate occasions without the leader's intervention. The leader's silence, to this teleworker anyway, almost validated the traditional employee's explicit jab but implicit stab—that teleworkers are lazy while everyone else works. After about six months, she requested and received a team transfer. This was the leader's failure.

Time and again, the great leaders, the ones that make telework work, manage impressions to create a team norm of fairness. They do so through impression management, one of the most understated and undervalued of all leadership skills. In looking at almost every case in which telework worked, we found leaders who influenced perceptions, particularly of those workers on-site in traditional assignments, so they could see, appreciate, and value the contributions of the teleworkers.

None of the requisite leadership actions were difficult or complex. For example, one leader would be sure to thank teleworkers in public and during conference calls. When awards season came along, these leaders often showcased at least one teleworker to let the rest of the team and other members of the organization know that teleworkers contribute in meaningful ways.

---

### WHOSE WORD COUNTS?

When we began the research and writing of this book, we came across one notable case at a rather large university. This university had two satellite campuses where students took coursework online, over tele-video, or through visiting professors from the main campus. Morale was low at these satellite campuses, and so were revenues and student applications. Faculty, staff, and students at these satellite campuses felt underserved, underappreciated, and undervalued. They were, after all, out of sight and out of mind. All that changed when a new dean entered the picture.

One of the lasting traditions of this university was to depart from the common practice of asking high-profile outsiders to speak at graduation. Rather, this university prided itself on selecting one or two of its own students for this honor. It made it feel authentic, personal, and warm. The new dean asked a simple question to the speaker selection committee: "When's the last time we had a speaker from one of our satellite campuses speak at graduation?"

"Never," came the response.

"You mean to tell me that in over 139 years, we haven't once had a speaker from one of our downstate partners?"

"Nope."

The dean stood up. "That changes today. No wonder they don't feel part of the team, part of the university. Involve them. They've got great students too. Let's spotlight that talent downstate. And maybe they'll appreciate us more and we'll be sure to value their contributions more too."

Wrapped in that decision were the leadership ideals of fairness and equity nicely wrapped in the leadership skill of impression management. From that point onward, the other contributing campuses weren't called "satellites," they were called "partners"—and things began to change dramatically.

## COORDINATE TEAM ACTIVITIES

To use an analogy, many of the best leaders of virtual teams could have been world-class travel agents. Like good travel agents, they knew the needs, desires, and wants of the people they served. More to the point, though, they were also great schedulers who were aware of time zones and differences. Time and again, we found that many virtual team leaders took their scheduling duties very seriously. Chances are a virtual team will have team members in several time zones. Scheduling across these time zones is difficult, especially if the goal is to minimize hardship for the team members. This requires leaders who can coordinate and schedule wisely.

*The very best leaders of virtual teams were also skilled schedulers and coordinators.*

Nothing makes a virtual team member more upset than meetings that aren't run well. Imagine getting up in Stockholm at 6:00 a.m. for a weekly meeting via conference call where all the other members are in the United States. The meeting goes on and on for almost two hours and at the end there's nothing to show for it. That isn't respectful or fair to the team member in Stockholm. Or to any team member, for that matter.

*As a leader, you have the responsibility and duty to run meetings well. Don't waste your team's time.*

Leaders grasp the importance of running effective and efficient meetings. What we observed in cases of making telework work were leaders who did the following:

- Established a clear agenda for each meeting.

- Kept to solid but flexible time guidelines for each agenda item.

- Canceled a meeting if there was nothing to discuss; there was never a case of having a meeting just to have one.

- Ensured that a dominant person never commandeered or hijacked the meeting.

- Made decisions based on the meeting—old items were hardly ever rehashed from meeting to meeting; decisions were made and the team moved on.

- Tended to discuss only important and relevant team priorities and action items.

- Sent or posted minutes or summaries within twenty-four hours of the completion of the meeting.

## DEVELOP A SIXTH SENSE FOR CONFLICT

Do you have a sixth sense? Great teleworking leaders do.

In classic clairvoyant style, leaders of virtual teams detect the seeds of conflict when few others could. We can't overstate the importance of this gift or skill; the hallmark of any great leader is to be able to manage team conflict. Without exception, conflict management is much harder in a virtual environment than in a traditional team mode. This is one reason why leading teleworkers can be more difficult than leading traditional in-house employees.

Consider the force of body language. Some researchers suggest that body language alone constitutes upwards of 60 percent of a given message. Smiles, frowns, groans, or winks all attach meaning to words. Often telework leaders aren't afforded the benefit of seeing—only hearing and reading. For those reasons, we found that the very best teleworking leaders possess highly tuned antennae directed at the moods, attitudes, and communication patterns of their employees.

Stop and think about it for a moment. This sensitivity involves real detective work. By no means is it easy, but it is necessary.

One of the better teleworking leaders that we talked with said that he looks for changes in e-mail patterns. For example, one of his teleworkers would write long e-mails with embedded cartoons and an inspirational quote at the bottom. One day, all the e-mails from this teleworker were short, without the cartoon and the inspirational quote. The perceptive leader saw this as a change in virtual behavior and picked up the phone, learning that the teleworker's fourteen-year-old cat had passed away the day before. On another occasion, the leader noticed that one of his teleworkers stopped using the first name of one of the team members in e-mail correspondence. She wouldn't address e-mails to this particular colleague by first name, but she would for everybody else. Again, he grabbed the phone and found out that this one employee was miffed that the colleague had failed to deliver on two deadlines and, because of that, caused her to miss a deadline. Another employee started to cc all on some e-mail traffic. The e-mail thread started to extend beyond five messages. Sensing some escalation, he set up a conference call between himself and the two employees. In each case, the leader's sensitivity made it possible to reinforce ties with team members.

If it isn't reading between the lines, it is reading lips. The most effective leaders of virtual teams become skilled at detecting tone of voice. People often ask us, "Is that it? Is that all leaders have to go with?" The answer is largely yes. Listening for tone of voice and reading text are the two detection tools you've got to gauge individual and team mood. It takes practice and patience. Often, the best thing you can do is check and verify. Be up-front and ask if you think you're sensing or feeling something. The guesswork needs to end early in leading telework to make it work. Take the time to ask the employee if your hunch is right.

*Listen and watch carefully for clues for conflict. Read between the lines. Handle problems early and swiftly before the virtual world takes over.*

Teleworking leaders don't have the luxury of reading body language. Instead, they rely on knowing the communication patterns of employees and a general sense of when things may go awry.

Great teleworking leaders are all cut from the same cloth. Not only do they sense when conflict is brewing, they initiate action plans to address the conflict. Again, the importance of conflict resolution is amplified in a virtual world. For starters, conflict can seethe and grow toxic more easily in virtual environments where detection is harder. Second, imagination comes into play to make toxicity worse. Whereas people sharing physical workspaces can verify and align words with body language to confirm meaning, that can't be done virtually. As a result, too many people read meaning into e-mails and mentally create something that may not even be there. Also, it is much harder to detect sarcasm or even a joke when no smile or laugh accompanies the words. The virtual world is a launching pad for miscommunication. Now, you might be thinking, "What's the big deal about a little miscommunication?"

On the surface and by itself, it may not seem like a big deal. But consider the fact that resolution can be difficult. In live and traditional offices, employees can walk over and verify and confirm almost immediately. That's harder to do when thousands of miles and five time zones separate them. Teleworking leaders at the top of their game grasp the importance of early detection and open communication in making telework work.

## MAKE IT PERSONAL

The ultimate litmus test of a teleworking leader is quite simple: Can the leader make the impersonal virtual world personal? When that feat is accomplished, the leader is barreling down the path to truly making telework work.

There's no easy solution here. Yet we've seen leaders employ creativity and empathy toward making it personal. As one of the more successful virtual team leaders we spoke with told us:

> *This is going to sound so like high school. But one of the more substantive things I did as a leader was to give our team a name. On Friday, we were just another virtual team. Just a collection of teleworkers. Over the weekend, I watched the Jack Nicholson movie about the "Jackal." On Monday morning, I asked for a team name. Online, we listed a bunch of virtual names and I put down "The Jackals." And it won. And forevermore and to this day that virtual team still identify themselves as Jackal 1, Jackal 6. It gave an identity to a faceless team. I miss the Jackals.*

And Keri, another virtual team leader with no physical interaction with any of her six teleworkers, found another way to make it personal. She sent virtual greeting cards when one of her team members performed well. Just as they would if they received a regular Hallmark card, her employees appreciated the gesture.

These are some remarkable but simple examples. Rooted in each case, though, is the use of a good-natured sense of humor. The e-cards were funny and reinforcing at the same time.

Another virtual team leader took a series of steps designed to make it personal prior to assuming her leadership role. Upon finding out that she was to be the new team leader, she spent the weekend creating virtual chat rooms for her team members. She also created online bulletin boards for people to post different thoughts and ideas—both personal and professional. She even went so far as to create a playroom in one of her team's newly created virtual rooms with online games and puzzles. Many would think this ridiculous. By all accounts, however, this leader earned the highest evaluations from her employees of any virtual team leader in the organization while placing in the top 5 percent for team performance metrics.

How did she do it? She did it by creating a team. She did it by creating an atmosphere of fun. She did it by creating a social feel along with the *Make it personal. Build a socially strong virtual team.* virtual touch of telework. More than anything, she did it by taking the virtual and impersonal and making it social and personal. She took it personally.

## UNDERSTAND TEAM MEMBER ROLES

While it may be a stretch to compare virtual teammates to actors on a stage, that's exactly the sense we got when we examined the most successful virtual teams. In these teams, the leaders proved exceptional at clearly identifying, assigning, and evaluating different roles for specific players. Again, the tension between generalists and specialists surfaces. Certain team members may fulfill general roles such as facilitator, tasker, or relationship builder. Still other roles may be more specific, such as timekeeper, reviewer, financial and cost controller, or recorder. As leaders contemplate the roles that they assign to their telework team members, they may wish to consult the work of Dr. Meredith Belbin, an expert in effective team behavior. In *Team Roles at Work*, she contends that the very best of teams are well balanced among the following roles: implementer, completer/finisher, monitor/evaluator, coordinator, investigator, and researcher. Wise leaders take stock and find out if these roles exist currently within their teleworking teams. If any are currently unfilled, they should be assigned to existing team members if possible—and if not, new team members who can fulfill these roles should be added.

Many leaders cement the importance of roles and role assignment through an initial performance counseling. In a sense, there's a communication element to it all. In the best teleworking teams, the members know their roles and the expectations that coincide with fulfilling those roles.

But it doesn't stop there when it comes to leadership greatness in a virtual team world. Not only was the leader good at communicating roles to the assigned individuals, these leaders were even better at telling the team members what role each of the others would play.

*Great leaders are skilled at assigning and communicating roles to the individual and to the whole team. They create a collective mind and a collective understanding.*

From this, effective interdependence arises—when the members each know their virtual role and the role of every team member around them. What this builds is a collective team mind—an understanding of the bigger picture. Predictably, when this transformation takes place, goal understanding and goal fulfillment move from the individual to the team level. This isn't cut and paste. This is a team with all members rowing in the same direction, all with a clear understanding of the destination. Above all else, it is about effective interdependence.

## BLEND VIRTUAL AND
## PHYSICAL INTERACTIONS

We are aware of a large university that conducted some research to see whether teleteaching worked. By and large, the results were favorable. A major finding of this institutional study revealed, however, that the best formula was a blended teaching format. We found similar suggestions when we talked to leaders that made telework work as it relates to teams.

A blended experience is a mix of virtual and physical interaction. For the university, it meant one hour of traditional, physical classroom experience for every three hours of virtual learning and interaction. Leaders who make telework work follow a similar equation for building great teams. When the budget allows, leaders get more of the five senses involved by getting the team members together. Instead of just reading and hearing, team members can attach a face to an e-mail address and a voice on a conference call. Remember, a core theme of this chapter is that a leader transforms the impersonal to the personal. Getting people to interact physically, at least occasionally, goes a long way toward that imperative. The virtual team members, the teleworkers, will feel part of a team because of the blended approach.

*If possible, pursue the blended approach. Physical interaction makes the virtual team stronger and more cohesive.*

Names, faces, and personalities all tend to come together when there's at least some physical interaction.

## FIND THE WEAK LINK

Not long ago, we shared some of our thoughts and research with a senior professor who used virtual teams for his MBA business strategy course. When the issue of interdependence arose, he nodded in agreement, saying,

> *It's never the missing link that brings down one of my MBA teams. Usually, it's the weakest link that brings everyone down. The weakest link is a lightning rod for conflict. Instead of my groups putting their cognitive energy into their project, they boil over, angry at the weak link. If I were to give one piece of leadership advice, I'd tell leaders of virtual teams to deal with the weak links.*

Clearly, this professor was on to something. In true interdependence, all members are tightly connected and integrated. There's some good and bad in that. We've talked about the good. The bad is the presence of a weak link. With a highly interdependent team, superstars can be brought down by duds.

For virtual teams, this issue is even more magnified. Our best advice, based on what we saw looking at effective virtual teams, is to put the detective hat back on.

*Any team is only as strong as its weakest link.*

Telework and virtual worlds give better cover to weak links, because poor performers can hide behind e-mail and phone calls. We've found that a general rule applies: It takes longer to identify weak links and poor performers in a virtual world. For these reasons, leaders must be on top of their game. They must have a constant finger on the pulse of individual and team performance. Attention to detail becomes an important leadership attribute here. The leaders who make telework work understand this simple truth. They respond by using a series of regular performance metrics to ensure that teams don't harbor stragglers. Leaders of teleworkers must ensure the pack is moving together. It is difficult to identify outliers if the leader isn't regularly tracking or being informed of performance progress.

*Leaders quickly identify weak links on their virtual teams because they track and monitor individual and team performance.*

## HARD DECISIONS

The Declaration of Independence declares famously, "We hold these truths to be self-evident." After about forty years of combined experience in leadership, we offer a truth that we believe—and can prove—really is self-evident. Truly great leaders, virtual or traditional, separate themselves by making (and then acting on) hard decisions. It takes resolve—and a strong stomach—to make the hard decision. In the end, this separates the truly great leaders from all others. The ability and will to make hard decisions is of particular importance when leading virtual teams. We wish the story ended with the identification of the weak link. It doesn't. To finish the job, great leaders move beyond just identification. They deal with the weak link.

---

### A WEAK LINK

Consider the case of Lindsey, an accomplished leader of virtual teams.

"Two weeks ago, I had to fire one of my teleworkers. I hate it. The Hollywood model makes the world think leadership is glamorous. I don't always think so. Sometimes it's just painful for me and for the employee."

Intrigued, we pushed. "What happened?"

"Well, our virtual team drafted up a team charter. There are only eight of us, and it took some time to draft this charter—essentially, the rules and roles we'd go by on our virtual team. One of the core elements in our charter was availability. We decided that for our team to be effective, we'd need to make ourselves readily available to each other and to our clients. Actually, we thought that was going to be our source of team competitive advantage. One team member joked that we were the 'first responders' of the virtual world."

"Go on."

"Initially, all went well. For example, we had an informal team rule that we'd answer all e-mails within six hours of receipt. For phone calls, one hour. If somebody called, we knew that it was relatively important, so we pledged to return calls in sixty minutes or less. You know, we were trying to build this culture of availability and responsiveness."

"Sounds like a great idea," we chimed.

"And it was. Seven of the eight team members bought into it. But one of our more important team members from a role perspective, our cost analyst, didn't buy in. He didn't play by the rules. His teammates would call and he wouldn't call back. He wouldn't return e-mail for days and often he wouldn't answer e-mail thoroughly. I'm the guy's leader and he wouldn't even return my e-mails or phone calls."

"Sounds like a train wreck approaching."

"It was. Because you can't force somebody to do something. Especially in a virtual world. This guy just closed up. Wouldn't return calls or e-mail. And we were all depending on him to provide cost estimates and budget analysis for several projects that we were working on. I almost waited too long. I could feel and sense that some of my teleworkers felt they were going to blow the deadline. All because one guy wouldn't do his job. I tried to counsel him over the phone and over e-mail and I documented everything. But he just simply stopped working. And so I had to fire him."

This conversation reflects an implicit understanding of leading virtual teams and making telework work. Team effectiveness is built on trust, reliability, and momentum. When a team member doesn't deliver, it can impair all three of these forces. Leaders must create and enforce a culture of responsibility and must be willing to hold team members accountable. As Lindsey noted, forcing a virtual team member to act can be difficult. There's no physical presence, no evil eye, no stopping by the cubicle to directly or indirectly spur action. For these reasons, leaders of virtual teams must build commitment and hold team members to a norm of commitment. Let us be clear about this last point—it's the leader who is responsible for creating and enforcing team norms. If the norm is availability, then it is the leader's duty to reward and enforce norms that reinforce the individual and team toward availability.

*Leaders who make telework work do two things particularly well—they make hard decisions, and they create and enforce productive team norms.*

## PROFILE OF HIGH-PERFORMING TEAMS

Not sure what an effective team looks like? The first thing we noticed in talking with many leaders and team members was that people were having fun; the team was happy. Leaders play a causal role in creating this happiness. As mentioned earlier, they can make the impersonal virtual world somehow personal. Obviously, this attitude is not confined to virtual teams. Effective virtual teams demonstrate some of the same habits as traditional teams. They can be creative, collaborative, and supportive. More important, they have tons of communication. Effective virtual teams and the leaders responsible for them communicate freely and often.

For the truly great teleworking teams, you'll find that the team members are absolutely clear why they exist, what their mission is, and what their shared goals are. The best virtual teams share this collective mind. They all know what the important stuff is, and they all tend to row in exactly that same direction. They have agreed-upon guidelines and procedures for making important decisions. As with Lindsey's team and its charter of availability, we found that the top-performing virtual teams all agreed on some basic ground rules and processes of how to operate. Of course, the leader has much to do with making that happen.

*Top-performing virtual teams love to communicate—and they know how to do it.*

Lastly, the team members will tell you that they feel part of the team. They will tell you that they feel appreciated by both the leader and their colleagues. Any team member who doesn't feel appreciated promptly begins looking for a way out. Leaders know this; they want their team members to stay in—to be

*Top-performing virtual teams know why they exist and where they are going together. They have consensus surrounding the ground rules.*

part of the team. A great way to do this is to just say "thanks" or "good job" and make the team members feel appreciated.

## GUIDING PRINCIPLES

This may not sound particularly sexy, but much of what we found in building and leading teams to make telework work was deceptively simple and straightforward. The very best of the virtual team leaders that we came across were able to strip away the clutter and noise to focus on the basics of leading teams. As we came to see personally, mastering the basics can take you and your team far.

*Forget about cut and paste.* Teams aren't just collections of individuals. They are people working together in the spirit of effective interdependence. Cutting and pasting your way to making telework work is impossible. Great teams are those that work interdependently—never independently. The difference between the two isn't three letters, it's the difference between success and failure.

*Diversify.* You don't have to be Warren Buffett to know that diversification works. Make sure you've got relationship-oriented people on your virtual team. They serve as the social glue for the task-driven members. Diversity will carry the day; seek a variety of learning styles, personalities, and backgrounds to fill out your team if you want to make telework work.

# GUIDING PRINCIPLES cont.

**Be fair.** Nothing will tear a virtual team up quicker than the perception of unfairness, inequity, and favoritism. Great leaders manage perceptions and ensure the notion of fairness is wired into the DNA of their team.

**Assign and communicate roles.** The very best leaders assign and communicate roles to both the individual members and the team as a whole. Leaders must also be willing to roll up their sleeves and deal with weak performers. One leadership law that no technology can ever erode is that authentic leaders make hard decisions.

**Make it personal.** If you pushed us to identify the defining characteristic of great virtual teams and the leaders of those teams, we'd say that these leaders made it personal. Through engaging communication, humor, and blended approaches, the top leaders were able to transform the dull, boring, and impersonal virtual world into one that was deeply personal, one where people *felt* part of a team.

# 5

# LEADERSHIP:
# THE CATALYST FOR CREATING
# A TELEWORK CULTURE

*No culture can live, if it attempts to be exclusive.*
**Mahatma Gandhi**

All organizations have a culture. However, *organizational culture* is an elusive term. It is an intangible concept that many have a hard time defining. Ask anyone in a given organization to describe what culture is, and they're likely to tell you that they can't specifically define it, although they can tell you if their organization's culture is good or bad. As a working definition, organizational culture can be thought of as the collection of beliefs shared by the members of an organization that distinguishes it from all other organizations. Think of it as the personality of the organization. And leaders mold that personality, by design or by accident.

---

### OUT OF SIGHT . . .

We stood with a business analyst of a midsized service company on the third floor at the company headquarters overlooking the parking lot. The sun was just starting to slip behind the treetops.

"You see those people?" the analyst asked us as he pointed to the trickle of people moving from the rear doors of the building into the parking lot toward their cars. "All of those guys are C performers."

### OUT OF SIGHT . . . cont.

The analyst was referring to the company performance evaluation system that assigned letter grades to employees: "A" ratings for top performers, "B" ratings for performers who occasionally achieved high results, and "C" ratings for mediocre performers.

"What do you mean?" we asked. We noticed the clock on the wall read 5:03 p.m.

"Easy," he said. "It's like watching Fred Flintstone jump off the dinosaur when the whistle blows at the end of the day. Those guys down there don't spend any more time at their desk than they have to."

The comments immediately piqued our curiosity. "You mean, in order to be ranked higher you have to work longer hours? What if those workers heading home accomplished a lot during the past eight hours? Or, what if they're going home and working a few more hours later that evening?"

"Doesn't matter. You can't expect to get very far here if you only work forty hours a week in the office. You have to be visible if nothing else. If people see you sliding in at eight o'clock and running out the door at five, then everyone will think you're a slacker."

We were almost afraid to ask the next question. "This company has a telework program, right?"

"Yeah, right," he laughed. "Sure, we have a telecommuting policy in writing, but who in their right mind would try to do it? It would be the kiss of death."

We were mindful that we were discovering the perceptions of a fairly junior employee. We were not interviewing an executive or senior member of management. We stood with one of the many analysts the company employs. We asked, "Does everyone feel this way?"

"Sure. My boss reiterates this to us over and over. It's just the way this company is, I guess."

Immediately we realized the importance of an organization's culture in making telework work. More important, we uncovered the leader's role in growing and cultivating organizational culture. Organizational culture can be a huge driver of successful telework, and culture originates from the organization's leaders.

# IDENTIFYING ORGANIZATIONAL CULTURE

To identify an organization's culture, a leader has to recognize what the organization truly values. Is the organization aggressive or does it value long-term stability? Is innovation and creativity encouraged or is risk taking frowned upon? Does the organization focus more on the end results or the process of achieving desired results? Is it people oriented or outcome oriented? Leaders need to understand how employees see the organization and not just what is printed in the formal vision or mission statements.

We realize that one size doesn't fit all, but in our experience, successful teleworking cultures have several things in common. The organizations tend to be more collaborative than directive. They value performance and are more outcome oriented than process oriented. Most have a spirit of innovation and are not afraid to experiment, take calculated risks, or suffer minor setbacks. They are comfortable with ambiguity and not having everything clearly defined or set in stone. Above all, these organizations cultivate a culture of trust and individual responsibility.

Correctly assessing the organizational culture is critical to making telework work. An organization's culture influences and reinforces behaviors without the need for formal documentation, written procedures, or published guidelines. Leaders will ultimately spend less time developing rules and regulations if the organizational culture is aligned with their intent. In today's work environment, where it's common to find firms with flat hierarchies, reliance on teams, and constant internal reorganizations to meet changing market needs, organizational culture can propel employees in a desired direction with less formalized structure. On the other hand, a company's culture can be a massive roadblock to change.

As we spoke with others in the business analyst's company, we started to learn more and more about the company's culture. Involuntary turnover in the company was high, especially among members of senior management. No one felt safe if they didn't meet the numbers. As one manager put it, "Here, you must always execute. Do whatever you have to, but just make it happen." The culture was outcome oriented to the extreme. In addition, the company also valued face time.

A widely held belief within the company revolved around the need to be physically present to get the job done. Others believed that not being physically visible made them vulnerable if things didn't go well. Employees regularly traveled across the country to attend meetings that lasted only a few hours. It was no surprise that teleworking would be a challenge for them.

Companies with a culture that emphasizes face time have a particular challenge implementing telework. In some cases, the company culture was clearly not in place to support telework but management went forward with a telecommuting policy or program. Most employees were afraid to take advantage of the opportunity and those that did quickly felt alienated. "It was supposed to be an incentive and a way to retain employees," one manager said. "In the end, it was neither." Part

*To make telework work, leaders should make sure the organizational culture will support it.*

of the problem was that telework was introduced as an initiative rather than the way the company should do business. The initiative was in direct conflict with the culture. To make telework work, leaders must first create a culture that supports telework by understanding that technology can be used to accomplish the job without the limits of physical presence.

## HOW LEADERS CREATE CULTURE

Leaders ultimately craft and influence corporate culture, whether intentionally or not. The behaviors and actions of leaders drive the behaviors of the organization. Leaders create the norms that permeate the company. In its simplest form, the basic concept is that leaders are the role models for everyone else.

Examining the service company in more detail, we noticed that no one in upper management took advantage of the new telecommuting policy. In fact, none of the senior managers lived outside the corporate headquarters location. Anyone moving into the senior ranks, whether by promotion or as a new hire, was simply expected to relocate to the headquarters. We asked one of the company's directors why no executives or senior managers lived outside the headquarters city even though the firm had operations in the forty-eight continental states.

"That would be impossible," he said. "How else could you interact with peers and senior leaders?"

This attitude summarized the corporate culture. Telework cannot be successful unless the leaders provide an example to the rest of the employees. In contrast, one Silicon Valley technology company we found demonstrated how leaders could create a teleworking culture. Its senior executives were dispersed across the globe, feeling no need to live anywhere near the company headquarters. Although some resided near a local sales office, others re- mained home-based and relied on a variety of methods to communicate with their em-

*Leaders must set the example to make telework work! Telework is not just an incentive program— it is the way to do business.*

ployees and supervisors. The company created some basic human re- source policies outlining telework arrangements but had never formally launched a telecommuting or teleworking program in its twenty-year history. Teleworking was regarded as how the company conducted business.

## NEW HIRE SELECTION: THE LEADER'S RESPONSIBILITY

In conversations with many hiring managers it's clear that selecting a potential candidate goes beyond job qualifications. Most of the hiring managers we spoke with admitted that they received stacks of résumés of qualified candidates and made their selection during the candidate interviews. Given qualifications that met the job description, many leaders chose candidates likely to fit in well with the company culture. Candidates with the same values, work styles, or work behaviors were offered positions over candidates with different attributes. Leaders in a culture that supports telework take this into account during the hiring process.

One hiring manager in a successful teleworking company re- counted, "I am a home-based manager, and the team I manage is scat- tered across the globe. In some cases, we only meet face to face twice a year. I happened to interview a candidate while I was traveling to the company headquarters. I interviewed two others over the phone. All were well qualified. I really liked the candidate I met and one that I interviewed over the phone. Which one do you think I picked?"

"The one you shook hands with?" we guessed.

"Wrong. I selected the one I never shared the same room with. I didn't meet him until several weeks after he started working. Although the candidate I did meet in person was strong, I didn't get a sense of his virtual presence. Think about it. The job required the employee to deal with people a continent or at least half the country away on a daily basis. Rarely would my employee have the luxury of sharing the same conference room with other members of the team. In our environment it's more important to me for someone to be good over the phone and by e-mail than to be good in person."

*Selecting the right candidates to come into the organization can have a huge impact on the existing culture, whether the leader is trying to change or reinforce it.*

Many managers would be reluctant to hire a candidate that they never physically met. However, corporate cultures that make telework work carry this over into all aspects of the business. Bringing new employees on board is one of the most critical, and sometimes most ignored, aspects of a leader's role. Filling the employee ranks with candidates who will telework well eventually reinforces the telework culture, creating positive and consistent employee behaviors.

## THE SOCIALIZATION PROCESS: HOW NEW MEMBERS ARE INTRODUCED INTO THE CULTURE

Drill sergeants for the U.S. Army and U.S. Marine Corps are fanatical about basic training—the initial weeks where recruits are transformed into soldiers. Every minute detail has been planned out at great length. It is a proven system that has evolved over hundreds of years. We don't advocate screaming at your new hires, imposing push-ups in the break room, or moving them at double-time between cubicles, but we do see the value in what is second nature for every drill sergeant: A successful induction process for new personnel is one of the most crucial stages of anyone's tenure with the organization.

After selecting the right candidates, leaders are responsible for the successful transition of the new employees into part of the company. This socialization process is when newly hired employees adapt to the company culture. New employees don't have the biases or opinions developed from years of working within the company walls. They're open to the knowledge and perspective provided by the leader. A brief window exists for the leader to positively influence new employees and help ensure their successful adjustment to the company.

The socialization process begins before new employees start working. In the army or marines, recruits are sent packets of information that inform them about the rigors of basic training and guidelines to physically and psychologically prepare them for the demands that will be placed upon them. Most organizations also mail welcome packets to new hires. Unfortunately, many of these welcome packets only contain basic facts about the company—salary information, medical and dental program information, confidentiality agreements, and the like. Corporate leaders miss a prime opportunity to learn from those in uniform and mentally prepare incoming personnel. To create a telework culture, leaders can use a variety of multimedia technology to engage new employees and set expectations before arrival.

Once new employees begin working, leaders can help them acclimate to the telework culture. Like the drill sergeants who carefully plan every detail in the military induction process, corporate leaders should consider a number of things in their environment. How are new employees introduced to the company? How do they meet other team members? Is there a training program to learn the business or specific job function? How is training delivered?

Returning to the services company struggling with telework, we studied the new-hire orientation program. Unsurprisingly, all new hires flew into the company headquarters for the two-day orientation class. The class was delivered by an instructor in a conference room with printed handouts and a PowerPoint presentation projected at the front of the room. This traditional approach differed greatly from that of the technology company, which had new hires log on to a site designed for incoming personnel, with specific videos and self-paced training content designed to help them learn about the company. Other remote team members arranged scheduled conference calls to introduce themselves to the new member using their webcams. Managers typically used collaborative software, such as WebEx, Cisco MeetingPlace, or Microsoft NetMeeting, to share the view of their desktop and walk the new employees through specific functions of their job. The leaders chose to use the technology in lieu of traditional methods, and this decision reinforced the telework culture with new employees.

Socialization does not necessarily end after the first week or even the first month. It is an ongoing process until the new employee becomes a self-sufficient and productive member of the team. Over time, the new employee will adjust and adapt to the company culture. Again, leaders can use this opportunity to strengthen the telework culture. Research suggests that programs that are formal, collective, and serial have a higher rate of success; however, do not confuse formal with traditional. The leader can continue to help the employee assimilate into the telework culture by employing technology to carry on the socialization process. At the technology company, employees participated in company meetings broadcast live over the Web, and consulted with others through instant messaging, wikis, conference calls, and e-mail—all of which supported the culture that telework was woven through the business.

> *The initial entry point for a new employee is one of the most critical times in the employee's tenure. Leaders must use this opportunity to ingrain the new hire into the telework culture.*

## SETTING EXPECTATIONS

Many leaders know the importance of communicating clear expectations to drive performance. The same principle also holds true for influencing corporate culture. It is almost passé to stress a company's vision and mission. Leaders, whether at the executive level or small team level, should also express the values that are important to them or their specific organization or team. We're not suggesting wallet-sized values cards or impressive presentations (although we've seen those work too); it's enough to tell employees in clear, concise, and concrete terms. If one of the key company values is teamwork, how does the leader translate this to the team? Simply tell people to work together? Or tell them that they're expected to record best practices from their individual projects and post them in a shared file? It's far more important for the leader to drive specific actions to cultivate a desired culture than to merely state lofty ideals.

There is a danger here if leaders do not explicitly communicate expectations. Organizations may inadvertently develop negative subcultures that counteract their efforts to create a telework culture. Many subcultures grow from the fault lines between departments or regions. Of course, subcultures aren't necessarily a bad thing for an organization. If a subculture is created intentionally by the leader or does not deviate from the larger organizational culture, then it can help propel the telework concept. U.S. Army units are famous for creating subcultures that are aligned with the overall mission of the organization. From Stetson-wearing cavalry commanders to airborne units, army outfits distinguish themselves from one another through their appearance, lore, combat history, and other shared experiences. But the real division among the units is based on their job function or combat role. This analogy carries over to the corporate world. For example, a large corporation may not advocate telework but a department head or midlevel leader could create a telework culture in an area that can use it.

> *Leaders must set clear, explicit expectations to create a telework culture. Beware of counter-productive subcultures that form without concrete expectations.*

---

### CHANGING CULTURE AT MARRIOTT

Bill Munck, a vice president at Marriott International, knows the importance of establishing clear expectations. Munck was confronted with the challenge of changing Marriott's culture of face time. Management believed that exceedingly long hours at the office and being visible was necessary for success. However, over time this philosophy made it difficult to recruit new managers, and some of the most talented managers, tired of putting in well over fifty hours a week on average, were leaving the company. Munck implemented a program he called "Management Flexibility" and revamped the way the employees thought about work.[1]

**CHANGING CULTURE AT MARRIOTT cont.**

Munck's efforts were not specifically tied to telework (although Marriott did include some telework solutions in the end); they were aimed at providing employees with better work–life balance. Regardless, the lessons learned in Marriott's culture transformation apply to telework. First, Munck created the perception that what he was implementing was actually aligned to the company culture. The company's culture was not only based on face time but was also aggressive and willing to try out new ideas. Munck initially positioned Management Flexibility as an experiment to help attract and retain top talent. The learning point for telework leaders is to tie telework into the existing culture. If the corporate culture is outcome oriented, leaders can demonstrate how telework will cut costs, drive productivity, or decrease cycle times. People-oriented culture? Show how telework will increase collaboration.

Munck also realized that skeptics and others would resist change. He followed up with personal meetings with managers to work through doubts or concerns. An outside consulting company then conducted extensive focus groups with employees, not only to gather feedback but to set the expectation that the company was serious about implementing the program. With feedback from the focus groups, the leadership team followed up with quick wins, addressing issues to build momentum and demonstrate that the leaders were executing. Published success stories broadcast the progress the company was making.

Telework leaders can take note of Marriott's strategy. After announcing the intent of incorporating telework in clearly defined terms, business leaders need to take action to reinforce the message. Identify and address people who may resist the change and reiterate expectations to them. Focus on small victories first to create momentum. And broadcast success.

*To increase adoption, leaders should show how telework supports the existing culture. Take action after expectations are set and concentrate on quick wins to build momentum.*

## IS THERE A DIFFERENCE BETWEEN
## A TELEWORK CULTURE AND
## A TELECOMMUTING CULTURE?

While speaking with leaders and teleworkers, we wanted to know if there was a telecommuting culture and how that differed from a telework culture. With the exception of a small consulting company where all the employees were home-based, we found that telecommuters almost formed a subculture within their company, and that, we believe, is one of the reasons why telecommuting has not been successful.

In some cases, telecommuting was created as an incentive program and offered to employees. However, the program was not linked to the existing company culture or senior management did not see the link between telecommuting and company goals. Telecommuting was thought of as an employee benefit, the opportunity to work from home, without benefits to the organization such as increasing productivity, reducing costs, or attracting and retaining top talent. A clear strategy of employing telecommuters was not developed. In other words,

*Successful telework cultures value results and teamwork without letting physical location get in the way.*

there were no clear, explicit expectations. The socialization process was weak, with nothing specifically addressing the needs or goals of telecommuters. Telecommuters were treated the same as office workers and then left on their own. As a result, telecommuters conversed with one another and developed an attitude that they were outsiders, not privy to the benefits of those working within the office cubicles. Office workers felt slighted too. Not understanding the challenges of telecommuting, they saw telecommuters as getting an unfair benefit of working from home.

The telework culture differs sharply from telecommuting because telework revolves around the concept of employing technology to achieve higher performance. Successful telework organizations valued results and valued teamwork but were almost blind when it came to perceiving an employee's physical location. For example, in one large company the company campus was so large that in a typical team meeting one team member might be at the opposite end of campus from another while a third teammate was three states away and a fourth member was working from home that day. The way the team interacted did not depend on who was at the company location, and no one had a false perception of other team members because they were not co-located at the company site.

Keep in mind that the telework culture does not mysteriously take root overnight. Leaders build the culture over time using a variety of tactics.

## THE LEADER'S TOOLKIT

Leaders have many tools that can be employed to create a telework culture. From the simple and inexpensive to the more complex, many techniques and tactics can be employed to increase the chances for success.

### Story Time

One of the simplest methods by which employees learn about the company's culture is through the stories shared by leaders during the induction process. Stories may contain narratives about the company's founders, success stories, responses to crisis, or management's reaction to mistakes. Leaders at any level can use storytelling to reinforce the company culture or transmit messages about the organization.

We asked one midlevel leader how he uses storytelling within his team. "I always enjoy showing the new folks a successful project we did not too long ago," he told us. "It was a true cross-functional effort involving teams from many areas of the company. Some were located here, other individuals were remote, and our development team was offshore. Most never even met each other face to face. The best part was that similar efforts had been tried in the past with no success. People began to believe we were attempting the impossible, but we beat our targets."

After the team was disbanded and moved to new projects, the manager posted the information to the company intranet, where new employees could read about the success and see the accolades senior management gave to the team. The important thing here is not necessarily what the project was about or how the leader used the intranet to record the project, it is the message he was trying to convey: A virtual project team surpassed its goal through collaboration and communication without the need to be in the same location. The leader's message was that telework worked.

Employees too will pass down tribal knowledge, information gained through their experience with the company, and they will also recount stories to new employees. Again, leaders should be forewarned about the subcultures that may exist within their organization's walls. The lore passed down from employee to new employee can thwart the leader's efforts toward teleworking. In an almost comical case, we encountered a company where the employees loved to tell new hires the story of their failed ERP implementation. With cynical glee, employees described how they worked seven days a week for months on end. Cots were set up in the conference rooms so teams didn't have to leave the building. Managers refused to let employees take out the empty pizza boxes that stacked high as snow mounds for fear of the trash carriers running past the dumpster and into their cars. Ambulances were called as a few individuals had nervous breakdowns at their desks. The message the veteran employees were sending to new hires was clear: We are not good at large-scale initiatives.

*Leaders can use storytelling as an effective way to create and reinforce a telework culture.*

Stories are powerful. Most of us can recall movie scenes better than we can remember facts or figures. The emotional impact of a story can weigh heavily in our psyche. A story passed to a new employee, or even to experienced employees, can be more meaningful than a full presentation full of charts and graphs. The leader can wield a story and convey a message that will be relevant even after the leader moves on. Storytelling is a potent tool that leaders should not overlook.

## Rituals

Organizational life is loaded with rituals, from the quarterly earnings meeting to the weekly staff meeting to the annual Christmas party. The consistent, repetitive sequences of activities employees participate in emphasize the organization's culture. Leaders can inject telework into existing company rituals or establish new ones to grow a telework culture. For example, do employees all gather in one location for the quarterly business update or annual earnings report? Conducting a company webcast or creating a podcast that employees could download at their convenience would add a telework aspect to this recurring event.

No activity is too small or too big to benefit from this principle. At one company we know, the team was split between the U.S. Eastern Seaboard and Hyderabad, India. They were already using weekly conference calls to join the halves of the team, the most primitive form of telework. The team members from India felt like outsiders. The conference calls were always scheduled in the middle of the night, their time, and some members couldn't participate. Simply rotating the times of the call or adding a webcam could have enhanced the experience. If a live meeting wasn't possible, then an online discussion board or a set of VODs (videos on demand that users can e-mail or download) could be used. Simple solutions that don't require large amounts of time or money can go a long way toward bridging the divide between teammates if used frequently. More important than the specific technology used is the creation of rhythmic sets of actions that communicate or express key values of the organization.

*By incorporating telework into repetitive activities, leaders can ingrain telework into the organizational culture.*

## Making Telework Tangible

Not only can leaders conjure up stories and create rituals to develop a telework culture, they can also use material symbols to support telework. It may seem counterintuitive that we suggest using something physical or tangible to support a virtual environment, but the physical environment is a powerful, although often ignored, source of influence. We take for granted the simple things such as an office layout, the size of a desk, type of office equipment, or placement of a chair, but the things around us that we can see and touch impact our behavior.

At the midsized service company we visited, we often heard complaints from senior managers that people from different functions didn't work well together. Employees didn't collaborate to solve problems. There was too much infighting among various groups. Remote workers felt alienated and never enjoyed coming into company headquarters. Some leaders shrugged this off as the price paid for working in such a results-oriented firm. Telework was not enabled for success because employees didn't work well together regardless of the medium or technology deployed.

One of the things we noticed was the office layout. Cubicles were arranged by department in different sections of the floor. The physical divisions between the groups was so apparent that you could easily tell when you left the land of the finance people and crossed the demilitarized zone into the area of the operations tribe. The "us versus them" mentality was easily recognizable. Ironically, management expected these teams to work in close conjunction with each other to achieve common goals. Employees rarely changed cubicle space, often occupying the same desk for years. People became attached to their physical space within the department. The higher someone rose through the organization, the larger the personal space became, until ultimately senior leaders would enjoy large, plush offices. And when workers flew in from the field, they found no seating space adjacent to their counterparts. Often, off-site workers were given an empty conference room to work from even if it was a floor or two away. Hardly anyone used the company's Web-based collaborative application, but that had less to do with the complexity of the software and more to do with the culture of the organization.

*Material symbols make a big impact even in the virtual world.*

The company that teleworked well had a different approach. The office layout was the type known as "hoteling." Gone were the dedicated offices and personal shrines of elaborate photograph collages adorning cubicle walls. The office floors were completely open. Employees arrived to work and selected a personal workspace they would use for the day. They plugged in their laptops, quickly logged in to the VoIP phone at each area, and began working. People chose to sit near people they needed to work with, not necessarily people in their department. Interestingly, the executive leaders, the vice presidents and senior vice presidents, sat in the open as well and not in private offices. Everyone was mobile to some degree. Employees felt more open with each other, worked better together, and found that they could easily approach others. Since physical location did not delineate divisions among employees, it was easy to see why they quickly adapted to telework.

## Carrots and Sticks—Using Rewards and Punishments

In Chapter 1 we discussed the leader's ability to influence behavior through both rewards and punishments. The same principles carry over in influencing company culture. All leaders have the ability to influence their culture through rewards; however, we caution about using rewards too often or rewarding outcomes that could have dangerous side effects. Leaders should use a reward (or punishment) system to change corporate culture as the last tool in the kit. Rewarding employees too frequently or rewarding behavior that is already common practice may lead to a feeling of entitlement and actually demotivate employees who were already doing what the leader wanted them to do. For example, one company we know gave employees cash awards when they cut money out of their budget. Employees began to expect the cash bonuses every time they reduced the budget, and those who didn't receive the bonus felt cheated. The irony is that many of these employees were from the finance, accounting, and purchasing departments that already had a mandate from management to reduce costs.

### Small Rewards

Leaders can avoid this trap by being selective about how and what they reward. First, small rewards can be just as effective as large rewards. Rewarding employee behavior does not have to come in the form of cash incentives, expensive plaques, or spectacular recognition ceremonies. Simple rewards can be just as effective. In one scenario, company management was encouraging process improvement efforts. Any team member who participated on a team that improved a process, regardless of the magnitude of the improvement, was invited to a quarterly lunch with the president. The president would walk around during the lunch, shaking hands with everyone and telling them what a great job they did. Employee improvement projects increased dramatically and employees began telling others with tremendous pride when they were invited to the luncheon. Additionally, the president created a competition. Due to the competitive nature of most employees, teams strived to have the highest number of projects involving the most employees. The prize was simply to be named as part of the best department.

*The symbolic meaning of an event can sometimes carry more weight than the reward itself.*

## Discretion

Leaders should be careful of what they are rewarding employees for. A distinction has to be made between the end result and the behavior itself. If, for example, you were attempting to increase the adoption of a new telework software application, how would you design the reward structure? The corporate culture is very traditional and does not adopt new technologies very

*Leaders can develop a rewards system to make telework work, but rewards should not be relied on as the sole method to influence the culture.*

well. Your immediate inclination is to reward the team or department that uses it the most. Perhaps you have metrics in place to measure how many times users log on or total time users have the application open. Does this really move you toward your intended goal of *adoption*? Most employees in this culture would quickly discover how to get around the system and hit whatever number was established as the goal. Users click on the application over and over or just remain logged in with no activity. A better system might be to award the team with the most creative use of the application. Again, the leader must balance the reward system with the intent or goal he is driving at. As the old saying goes, "People do what they are measured for, so be careful what you measure."

## Inverse Rewards

Lastly, leaders can set up the inverse of the reward system and punish undesired behavior. Another word of caution here when using punishment as a means to change culture: The leader should clearly recognize the chance that the attempt will backfire. Punishing those who don't conform can create negative subcultures that may eventually work against the leader's efforts. Sure, extreme cases of nonconformance or subversion should be dealt with harshly, but remember that in many cases the threat of punishment is enough. A vice president we know wanted to use telework technology to reduce department travel expenses. During a department meeting he stood up in front of all his employees and said, "I just want everyone to know where they stand in regards to travel expenses. This is not a hit list. It's for informational purposes only." He then showed a slide with all the teams in the department and their travel expenses for the quarter in rank order from most to least expensive. Included in the list were the personal travel expenses of the directors and managers. No disciplinary action was needed. Everyone got the message.

Like many of the other methods described in this chapter, rewarding or punishing employees can have a big impact on changing the organization's culture. However, there is more risk *As a last resort, the* with this method than with any of the other techniques discussed. Leaders should pay careful attention and understand the implications when developing a reward system. A poorly designed reward structure can have the opposite effect of what is intended and should only be used after other practices are already in place.

*As a last resort, the leader has the option of punishment to change behavior.*

## THE ONLY THING EASY
## ABOUT CHANGE IS SPELLING IT

Woodrow Wilson once said, "If you want to make enemies, try to change something." Organizational change is one of the leader's most difficult tasks. Anyone who has tried to change behavior—whether of an individual or a large organization—understands what a challenging task that can be. People may naturally resist change, and they may have hidden agendas, competing priorities, or not-invented-here mentalities. Changing or creating a corporate culture to support telework can be an uphill battle. It doesn't matter if you're the CEO or a midlevel manager, the challenges are the same, just at different levels. Some may believe that culture transformation is only possible through reactions to crisis or turnover in senior leadership. Others argue that culture change is only possible if the organization is small or is young enough to have no entrenched dominant beliefs. Although these all factor in to changing organizational culture, they do not prevent change. Moving to a telework culture is possible.

The organizational culture may dictate how readily the organization will adopt telework. Leaders at any level can employ our strategies and tactics to make telework a reality. What if you're not an executive? The telework culture can be created within the team. What if you're an individual contributor and not a people manager? No worries. We have met employees with no direct reports who were still able to influence the culture toward telework. By being the first to adopt a technology and demonstrating how it could be applied in new ways to cut costs or increase productivity, they were able to convince others to change their mind-set.

## GUIDING PRINCIPLES

Don't underestimate the power of organizational culture when it comes to making telework work. However, leaders at any level can change or at least influence the culture of their organization. Identifying what type of culture characterizes the organization is the first step toward creating a telework culture. Almost any culture can support telework; it is up to the leader to identify what is really important to the organization and how telework can help accomplish those goals. By applying some key leadership principles and strategies, leaders can help transform their culture.

***Be a role model.*** One of the fundamental tenets of leadership is to lead by example. Leaders cannot expect to create a telework culture without jumping in with both feet and leading the effort through personal example. Experiment with technology, be open to new ideas, and lead virtually as well as in person.

***Get the right people on board.*** Organizational culture is rooted in the minds of the people who make up the organization. Bring in the right mix of team members from outside and inside the organization— people who are inclined to support telework.

***Transform new personnel.*** The period when someone first enters an organization is the best time to enlist them in the corporate culture. Because new hires and others new to the organization do not have preconceived notions or biases built up from years of personal experience with the organization, they are more open to new working arrangements. Maximize this opportunity by incorporating telework into the socialization process and making it the way everyone does business.

# GUIDING PRINCIPLES cont.

**Set clear expectations.** Be explicit when setting expectations with your team. Translate the values of your organization or team into action steps that the team can execute every day.

**Tell a good story.** Storytelling is a powerful tool for leaders to get their message across. A story expressing the values of the organization can be more effective than a parade of PowerPoint slides or reams of data.

**Create your own rituals.** Creating consistent, repetitive activities involving telework can also help leaders instill desired values into the company culture. No task is too big or too small to use to advance telework.

**Don't forget the physical environment around you.** The physical work environment can also have a strong influence on telework. Don't ignore or take for granted simple things such as the office layout or equipment used by employees.

**Create a rewards system.** It may seem obvious to state that a rewards system can impact employee behavior. But it's important to understand how to create an effective rewards system—being selective on what to award and rewarding the right behaviors, not just outcomes.

# 6

# ACCELERATORS:
# TINY LEADERSHIP VARIABLES
# WITH HIGH IMPACT

*Give a man a fish, and you have fed him for today. Teach a man to fish, and you have fed him for a lifetime.*

**Anonymous**

We've heard this quote about a thousand times—and we still don't buy into it completely. For one, we offer our own fathers as evidence to the contrary. They've both tried to learn to fish and have had guides try to teach them to fish for the better part of five decades. But if our families had depended on our fathers' learning to fish, we'd be dead. And, joking aside, while people are learning to fish—while they grab hold of new principles—they still need to eat *now*. This chapter and the next one are less about policy, theories, and principles, and more about application, about making the leap from theory to practice. Because we know that sometimes you can't wait to eat until after you learn to fish.

To bridge the gap, leaders have access to several tools we call *accelerators*. These are tactics and strategies that help make telework work now while people learn to apply the underlying principles in their fully developed form.

## LEADER ACCELERATOR 1:
## COUNSEL EMPLOYEES

Sadly, initial counseling and performance counseling are rarely part of the telework introduction process. And when companies make the attempt, the results usually lack the true performance punch that counseling can deliver. Initial and performance counseling ought to be done whether employees are teleworking or not, of course. But we feel that it's absolutely essential that leaders counsel their employees when it comes to telework.

Counseling is important because it affirms expectations and reduces miscommunication. Employee counseling has several basic tenets that should spark and lead to teleworking success. Counseling is about communicating and revisiting goals and objectives. It is about clarifying standards, ground rules, and expectations. Also, counseling offers a voice to the employees and it's where the leader can learn what is going well and what can be improved.

Many feel that employee counseling is a one-way activity. Hardly. The best leaders are counselors who listen as much as they talk, or more.

For this leader accelerator, we suggest conducting formal initial counseling and then scheduling a counseling session every quarter, at a minimum. In between, the leader can engage in informal counseling. Trust us when we say that telework works best when counseling is there to support it.

## LEADER ACCELERATOR 2:
## FORMALIZE AGREEMENTS

Hollywood leadership is sexy and glamorous. Real leadership means getting into the trenches and getting dirty. An area where the leader should get dirty—"get administrative"—is enforcing a telework agreement with signatures from both the leader and the employee. This applies to traditional telework assignments where employees could be working remotely hundreds of miles away or to local employees who work from home every so often. This formalized agreement should be no more than three pages, but should dovetail nicely with what we discussed in regard to counseling—it formalizes the ground rules of the telework arrangement. This agreement should specify where in the home or elsewhere the telework should occur and should probably address the hours that a teleworking employee is expected to work.

A good agreement should be reviewed by legal counsel for several reasons. First, the leader needs to protect all three parties: the employee, the leader, and the organization. An agreement then should indemnify or hold harmless the leader and employer if something out of the organization's control occurs in the home office. For instance, we came across a story where a teleworker's three-year-old toddler came into the home office and promptly tripped. She fell into the corner of a desk with a sharp edge. The desk corner missed her eye by about ten centimeters. The girl had to get fourteen stitches between her eye and her eyebrow. The teleworker did not sue the organization, but that was a personal decision—there was no signed agreement to protect either the leader or the organization.

*Remove the confusion and protect yourself— design a teleworking agreement.*

In addition, a teleworking agreement could address such things as employee leave laws, employee rights laws (including drug testing), worker's compensation, and unemployment. This is particularly important as states vary on all these laws. Because of the differences in state regulations and policies, leaders should recognize that one size doesn't fit all. Agreements should be at least partially specific to the worker's location.

## LEADER ACCELERATOR 3: DRAFT A TELEWORK TEAM CHARTER

A team charter goes beyond the individual telework agreement in reinforcing expectations, roles, responsibilities, and goals. Team charters are not meant solely for virtual teams but work for traditional teams as well. We've personally been on teams where a charter was drafted within the first ten days that the team formed. We can't say if our team success can be attributed directly to the fact that we drafted up a charter. Regardless, and whether by coincidence or by design, we can say with full confidence that teams that drafted and enforced their own charters were better performers.

There's no magic formula or template for a team charter. Most of what we've seen has been remarkably simple, concise, and to the point.

Typically, a team charter is one page long and spells out what the team's mission is, basic and core expectations for team operations, specific roles each team member is to adopt, and goals or outcomes that will determine whether the team is successful or not. We further recommend that this charter be posted consistently, front and center, on some type of Web portal. A team charter isn't that much different from our U.S. Constitution. It establishes the rules to work. The better leaders will refer to the charter as a source of strength and security and point to it as something that team members can rally around.

*Draft up and then rely on a team charter to guide work behavior and to inspire team members.*

## LEADER ACCELERATOR 4: PROVIDE THE RIGHT SERVICE AND SUPPORT

Del Perdew provides information and technology support for the forty-five or so faculty housed in the College of Business at Frostburg State University. He is a walking, talking help desk. At any time, for any problem large or small, Del is there to help and assist the faculty. He is patient and customer focused, and he explains technology in a way that is not intimidating. Del is a big reason why telework works at Frostburg State University. We've personally heard many professors say they wouldn't do online courses if it weren't for Del. In this is a lesson—a leader accelerator.

Leaders provide support and resources for their workers to succeed. As a leader, make sure you budget and invest in quality service and support. Knowing that service and support is there provides comfort and reduces anxiety for those thinking about teleworking. Leaders should also consider the type of support that will be offered. For example, if teleworkers will be working from home offices, will the company help desk be able to assist teleworkers or will they be responsible for troubleshooting their own home office equipment problems?

In today's world, teleworkers are obtaining a wide variety of consumer technologies—from iPhones to flash drives to digital cameras—all of which may serve a legitimate business purpose. Home-based workers may use their own routers and modems. To complicate matters, teleworkers may rely on a number of applications downloaded straight from the Web, such as statistical software for business analysis or Adobe Acrobat to review documents, which may or may not be supported within the existing IT infrastructure. If they can't count on support, or at least under- *Budget and invest in IT* stand what can or cannot be supported, telework- *service and support.* ers will become less effective. Also, if you do hire people for the help desk, make sure they've got strong interpersonal skills like Del. Nobody wants to call for IT support if the support isn't friendly and customer focused.

## LEADER ACCELERATOR 5: IDENTIFY AND RECOGNIZE CHALLENGES

Beyond providing resources and support, leaders should help their teleworkers identify potential problems and develop contingency plans or mitigation strategies to deal with these issues. We're not just talking about technical issues; you need to address personal challenges as well. Many teleworkers we spoke with were initially excited to work remotely or from a home office only to find that it was much harder than they ever anticipated.

"Working from a home office is difficult," one teleworker told us. "I initially thought I would have much more flexibility and could be around my family more. But I've tried to do early morning conference calls with my six-month-old daughter in one hand and the phone in the other. It just doesn't work."

The misperception is that teleworkers can work from home and multitask by simultaneously tending to personal matters. Unfortunately, attempting this sort of multitasking is both ineffective and inefficient. Leaders can help mitigate this problem by initially working with teleworkers to identify potential distractions while brainstorming potential solutions. For example, are kids, pets, roommates, or family likely to be tempted to enter a home office? If so, is there a local office or some other nearby location to ensure minimal disruptions? Can the home office setup be moved out of the living room and into a fairly soundproof room with its own door? By simply asking questions, the leader can encourage the teleworker to think through various scenarios.

Living in a different time zone presents challenges as well. One teleworker described the benefits of working from Texas when most of the company was based on the West Coast. He told us, "I get a couple of extra hours in the morning before most of the company wakes up. But conducting meetings at eight o'clock in the evening at my house can be hard."

Again, the leader can help the teleworker think through likely challenges. Are there recurring meetings at late hours? Is the company expectation that the employee will be available at certain times? Is it acceptable to shut down for certain hours of the day? Can a teleworker in a different time zone work offline for certain hours?

Technical issues should also be considered in the initial discussion. What happens when teleworkers lose connectivity because their local service provider has encountered problems such as a power outage? If the teleworker is using a particular technology to communicate that is not supported by the company's IT staff, what happens when that technology is not available or experiencing problems? What backup systems or locations are available to maintain productivity? After the leader and teleworker identify the risks and solutions, they can revisit the plan during quarterly counseling sessions to validate whether the strategy is working.

*Identify potential distractions or problems and develop contingency plans to mitigate these issues.*

## LEADER ACCELERATOR 6: FORMALIZE A MENTORING PROGRAM FOR TELEWORKERS

In the late 1970s, the *Harvard Business Review* released the results of a survey aimed at hundreds of senior executives. One of the key findings of this survey was that their professional success would never have occurred without a mentor along the way to help them to the top. What applied more than thirty years ago to senior executives applies today to teleworkers. Leaders mentor or find mentors for their teleworkers to optimize both their happiness and their performance.

Teleworking is not always easy both personally and professionally. Because colleges tend not to teach teleworking classes or management classes aimed at teleworkers, learning the ropes of effective teleworking can be difficult. While we've detailed many principles, lessons, and specifics, we have no doubt that we've missed things that could lead to teleworking success (or failure). It is the mentors, the ones who've done it before, who fill in the learning gaps. It is the mentors who answer the questions, who lend a helping hand, offer encouragement, and provide comfort. Teleworking is a lot like roaming into the frontier of the working world. Most early settlers didn't pioneer the frontier alone. They traveled in groups or had a guide. As a leader, either guide or find a guide or mentor for your teleworkers. Don't force it upon them, but make a mentoring program visible and available for them to take advantage of when they see the need.

> *Mentors and a mentoring program can increase performance and happiness of teleworkers.*

## LEADER ACCELERATOR 7: REWARD AND PUBLICIZE BEST PRACTICES

In earlier chapters, we discussed the leader's ability to influence teleworkers, teams, or the company culture through rewarding behavior. The same concept applies to the detailed procedures. The key here is to identify and look for effective teleworking behaviors to reward publicly, so as to encourage the teleworker to achieve higher performance and instill the same expectations in the entire team. When leaders do this, other teleworkers clearly understand what is desired and can change their behavior to match the leader's expectations.

> *Leaders should look for opportunities to reward and publicize specific teleworking behaviors.*

Within every team, some individuals will rise quickly, outperform other team members, and be rewarded in some fashion. The key is to specifically call out certain ideal teleworking behaviors so the rest of the team can learn. For example, in one nonprofit where e-mail was the predominant method of communication between teams, one manager struggled with how to get information out faster than just sending a PowerPoint file. One team member learned how to record and e-mail a simple video-on-demand (VOD) presentation with narrated slides. The manager not only thanked the creative team member publicly but also explained in detail why the idea was so powerful: It experimented with new technology to address a common issue. The rest of the team quickly got the hint. They were encouraged and expected to find new ways of doing common activities.

## LEADER ACCELERATOR 8: DEVISE AN EXIT STRATEGY

We've come across way too many cases where an employee thinks teleworking will be a cakewalk only to learn otherwise. Some employees think it's easy. Some think that they're just built to telework. Often, they think wrong—and that's okay.

Leaders, though, should know going in that not all employees who sign up to telework will enjoy it or perform well at it. For these reasons, leaders should develop an exit policy for those who wish to come back to a traditional work assignment. Granted, there may be cases where employees cannot return to their original traditional work environment.

*Anticipate the possibility that telework won't work, and devise an exit strategy in advance.*

Nonetheless, it's always useful to provide several exit options for the teleworking arrangement if it doesn't go right. The leader must then communicate those options to all workers.

We'd go so far as to recommend budgeting and planning for a 10 percent failure rate. Telework just isn't for everyone who tries it, no matter how good the selection tools are. The very best leaders and organizations are those that accommodate their employees—that are able to offer some flexibility. Leaders should never want employees to feel trapped or boxed in. So work with other leaders and possibly with your HR department to make sure that an exit policy is created that would allow employees to return to a traditional work arrangement if, for some reason, telework doesn't work for them.

# LEADER ACCELERATOR 9:
# PROTECT AND SERVE

Too many leaders have let informational and proprietary security slip on their watch. Don't be one of them. And for all the benefits of teleworking, one of the greatest risks is the loss of critical information. In a knowledge economy, protecting information may be even more important than protecting physical assets. An organization's competitive advantage can often hang in the balance.

Because of this, leaders should budget both time and money to the mission of security. What this means is that on a quarterly basis, leaders should evaluate the teleworking security program. We know of some leaders who do a mini-audit every three months. This includes evaluating the virus and security software and ensuring all teleworkers download all the latest updates. Password procedures should be clear for all teleworkers, along with how to handle sensitive information whether on paper or stored on laptops or removable drives.

*Keep an eye on security. A security breach could end the teleworking program regardless of its benefits to the organization.*

This last point is significant. While many organizations control access to the corporate facility, they are rarely aware of who is going into and out of people's homes. With a mobile workforce, information can be carried to unsecured areas or lost. In a recent survey by iBahn, a company that provides secure broadband services, travelers typically carry an average of $525,000 worth of sensitive information on their laptops—and 39 percent of survey respondents had experienced some type of virus or theft.[1] The risk is very high, but disaster is preventable. Leaders should ensure they partner with their IT counterparts to develop a security strategy. How will teleworkers get into the company network? Will teleworkers have to use digital certificates, hardware or software tokens, or encryption? Will teleworkers have access to all databases and applications?

Outside the IT and legal departments, some leaders may not be aware of all the security elements that are needed to protect the organization and the employee. Leaders should at least consider the risks by asking questions up front and developing a joint security strategy between IT, legal, and HR. Regardless of the specific security technology employed, the leader is responsible for establishing a plan and discussing it with the employees. One leader we know specifies information handling procedures in the teleworking agreement, discusses them during counseling, and verifies their use via mini-audit. This may seem overcontrolling. We see it as due diligence. We see it as leading.

## LEADER ACCELERATOR 10:
## MOVE AWAY FROM HARD DRIVES

For teleworking to work, information generally needs to be easily accessible and available to other members of the team—both traditional and virtual. We recommend de-emphasizing the use of local hard drives. Instead, leaders should emphasize network drives. When leaders do this, they improve the chances of strong teamwork while simultaneously protecting security. The real future of teleworking is not the computer but the network. Large bandwidths will allow streaming video and voice and allow for the dissemination of huge quantities of data.

*Consider using network drives for teleworking and information storage; it improves teamwork and security.*

Teleworkers should be instructed to put a version of all their work on network drives. This allows many people to access and comment on the information. When work stays on a single computer hard drive or flash drive, an information silo is created. Generally speaking, such silos stifle information sharing and collaboration. Shared folders on a network drive prevent this from happening. Also, security is one of the few areas where centralization may be preferable to decentralization. It is hard for a leader to enforce exact security standards and procedures across, say, a hundred teleworkers and the information they carry. However, organizations can more easily safeguard information when it is on the network server.

## LEADER ACCELERATOR 11:
## BECOME A PILOT

Teleworking is working against a tide of history dating back thousands of years—really, since *Homo sapiens* began to work. For thousands of years, the assumption was that you needed a physical presence to get work done. It shouldn't be surprising then that the largest obstacle facing telework is history and tradition. For precisely these reasons, we suggest changing DNA deliberately in a crawl, walk, run fashion.

We've found the best way to do this is to conduct a pilot or trial study first. Pilot or trial studies benefit the employee, the leader, and the organization. But pilot studies work only when accompanied by a heightened sense of awareness and observation. For instance, we know of one company that launched a six-month teleworking pilot study but never followed through. At the end of six months, neither the employee nor the leader knew if it was something worth continuing.

The entire rationale for conducting a pilot study is to observe and learn, to gather information that would fine-tune and improve the teleworking arrangement. Of course, this requires observation, evaluation, and analysis. The best teleworking leaders follow the military's After Action Review (AAR) process to ensure that the employee, the leader, and the organization capture lessons learned. An AAR is nothing more than discussing and documenting what is going well and what needs improvement. Some organizations use survey software to capture feedback from an AAR. Ideally, all parties should know whether they want to pursue a teleworking arrangement and what modifications need to be made to improve it. We suggest that for most organizations and most teams, a six-month pilot study is long enough and that an AAR should be conducted every two months during the pilot study.

*Do a pilot study; it will help you learn.*

## LEADER ACCELERATOR 12:
## DIY (DO IT YOURSELF)

When we looked at all the successful leaders of teleworkers and compared them to the ineffective ones, an interesting theme emerged. Very simply, the leaders who teleworked themselves were more effective than those who never did it, never tried it.

Leaders who have actually done telework before seem to gain a level of empathy and competence that informs their leadership decisions and choices. Teleworking may be such a foreign concept that you have to try it before you can lead it. There's an old Army mantra that seems to speak to this issue—*As a leader, how can you expect your follow-ers to follow if you haven't done it yourself?* The classic lead-by-example philosophy is at work here.

We recommend that leaders telework for at least six months before attempting to lead teleworkers—not necessarily just before launching the main telework program, but at some point in their careers. That's just long enough to give a realistic taste of the challenges and opportunities that accompany telework.

*As a leader, you must try telework at least once in your career. It buys you empathy and legitimacy.*

An interesting benefit surfaces and is be-stowed on the leader by the followers—that of legitimacy. Teleworkers seem more able and more willing to listen and follow a leader who has teleworked before. Such leaders are seen as "one of us," gaining some instant credibility. If you've never tried tele-work, a follower running into problems is apt to think, "You just don't understand. How could you? You've never done it before." That state-ment can never be leveled at leaders who have tried telework at least once during their career.

## LEADER ACCELERATOR 13:
## USE COMMON SOFTWARE AND HARDWARE

Revisiting our discussion of the concert conductor, we found that in cases where telework really hummed along, most teleworkers and tra-ditional workers were on the same sheet of music. And we mean this almost literally—they may not be reading musical notes, but they're sharing all the essential tools and information that they use.

Leaders are responsible for creating a context where people can work together easily, seamlessly. One of the most practical ways to pro-mote this kind of connection is to make sure that all teleworkers (and traditional workers, for that matter) use the same software programs and versions. For instance, we came across one publishing firm that employed teleworkers all across the country. We asked how it was so successful in creating such a dynamic and collaborative teleworking arrangement. Remarkably, one of the teleworkers brought up the point that there were no seams, no barriers. When we pushed more we learned that it was a company mandate that all employees use the same version of Word, the same version of Windows, the same version of Adobe, the same version of Office, and the same version of Outlook. This made everybody's job easier as the help desk knew what the common platform was for everybody. Sharing information was also easier since all workers used the same software. This organization even pushed this mentality to hardware, specifying which computers and printers and modems their teleworkers could use and which ones they couldn't. What's more, when a new software version came out, the rollout was usually done in a shock-and-awe fashion—it happened all at once, usually, over a weekend. The firm tried to avoid incremental upgrades. All these efforts made it easier for teleworkers to communicate and share information—the lifeblood of telework.

*When possible, adopt common software and hardware.*

## LEADER ACCELERATOR 14: USE ALERT ROSTERS

As mentioned earlier, a key common theme in telework greatness is the notion of accessibility. The best teleworkers and telework teams manage to make themselves available to other virtual or traditional workers.

This is a relatively simple tactic. It doesn't sound earth-shattering, and we know it. But we found its use consistently in great telework teams. As much as possible, leaders should create, update, and disseminate telework alert rosters or directories. There are two purposes to this—one overt, the other more subtle.

Alert rosters or directories make it easier to reach any specific teleworker. A good alert roster for teleworkers should have each one's full name, full position, immediate supervisor, home department or division, phone number, e-mail, fax, and time zone. We recommend the alert roster be updated quarterly to account for personnel changes and new hires. The alert roster should then be posted both electronically and physically. This is the overt rationale for using alert rosters.

*Create and distribute a telework alert roster.*

The more subtle reason for developing alert rosters and then disseminating them widely is to keep teleworkers visible within the organization. Oftentimes, we get feedback from both teleworkers and traditional workers that teleworkers can be ignored or forgotten. Publishing alert rosters reminds the greater organization that teleworkers are alive and well and are working hard.

## LEADER ACCELERATOR 15: APPRAISE PERFORMANCE AND BECOME METRIC FOCUSED

The entire premise behind telework is a leadership and management mind-set. When leaders or organizations embrace teleworking, what they're really saying is something like this: *We trust our employees and we're not particularly interested in how or where the work gets done—we just want it done right and to an exceptional standard.*

We couldn't agree with that premise more. But assumed in this mind-set is that outcomes and results take precedence over processes. To know whether a teleworker is effective or not, performance must be formally measured. We'll even go so far as to say, don't even think about launching into telework if you aren't willing to capture and assess performance all the time.

This point supports the first accelerator, performance counseling. Leaders need to appraise and measure performance regularly. We suggest weekly, monthly, and quarterly evaluations of performance. Leaders must take a further step and address performance metrics and benchmark telework performance based on these metrics or standards. At the end of the week, month, or quarter, the leader should know whether each teleworker and teleworking arrangement is working or not. Assessing performance early and often makes it possible to intervene early if a problem begins to manifest itself. One of the better teleworking leaders we saw had weekly performance discussions with her teleworkers. Remember that teleworking is predicated on delivering results and outcomes; it is impossible to deliver results and outcomes unless both the leader and the teleworker know the performance metric in the first place.

*Generate performance metrics and use them to continuously evaluate performance.*

We don't want to overstate this point here. But we will: In almost every case of teleworking failure, performance appraisal systems were conspicuously absent.

## LEADER ACCELERATOR 16:
## MAINTAIN STANDARDS

The decisions, actions, and behaviors of leaders are on display and open for public comment—leaders are under a microscope all the time. Nowhere is this more evident than in telework.

Leaders should strive to maintain standards evenly across teleworkers and traditional workers. If leaders fail to do this, perceptions of hypocrisy and favoritism can take root. This is so elemental to leadership that we almost didn't mention it. But after reflecting on conversations with teleworkers and their respective leaders, we see that one of the greatest forces working against telework and teleworkers is the perception of favoritism.

*Maintain standards evenly.*

Fight this perception problem. If it is unacceptable for a traditional worker to miss or be late to a meeting, the same standard should apply virtually. The greater the difference between conventional or traditional standards and telework standards, the less likely telework is to work.

## LEADER ACCELERATOR 17:
## SCHEDULE TIME FOR
## TELEWORKING RELATIONSHIPS

Did you know that most of the conversation within any organization is spontaneous and informal? Sure, there's a ton of meetings. In between meetings, though, people bump into each other, and they talk. They talk about work. They talk about hobbies. About sports. About families. One of the limitations of virtual work, of telework, is that there is no accelerator, no physical interaction, to spark simultaneous conversation. This is one obstacle a leader faces when managing teleworkers.

Leaders must build relationships with their teleworkers. It is impossible to do that without talking to them. And because they are out of sight and there's no chance for physical spontaneous interaction, leaders must go to certain extremes to make sure that the communication happens.

This may seem like the antithesis of spontaneous communication, but leaders of teleworkers often schedule time to talk and discuss matters with their teleworkers. One of the more successful leaders we talked to programmed time into his Outlook calendar for both formal and informal conversations with his teleworkers. His rationale was simple: "It's like a date with your wife. We get so busy. Overwhelmed. If you don't schedule it, if you don't program time for it, it'll simply never happen." Recall that a critical variable in making telework work is to communicate well and often. This is done when we earmark and set aside time to do so.

> *Communication is so important to teleworking that you may need to schedule it to make sure it happens.*

## LEADER ACCELERATOR 18:
## RETHINK INTERACTIONS

Picture your typical weekly staff meeting. You are in a conference room with your manager and your coworkers. A few of your coworkers are teleworkers or on the road and are calling in to the meeting. Your manager runs through an agenda, coworkers give brief updates on their respective areas one at a time, there's some discussion, and finally a recap before the meeting ends. The coworkers on the phone are largely ignored, or if there is a discussion they usually can't be heard over the conversation in the room. They only speak when spoken to. After the call, the employees in the conference room don't feel the value of those attending the call and those not in the room feel alienated or forgotten.

Leaders should be aware that things change slightly in a teleworking world, and should be prepared to adjust their tactics accordingly. In a meeting, the fundamentals may not change—having a clear agenda, taking minutes, providing a recap before closing—but the techniques to engage all the participants do. With people meeting virtually, verbal cues are more difficult to pick up and there's no body language to respond to. A leader in this case may have to send out specific information beforehand and point out where input may be needed. Members not physically present may have to be called on specifically to ensure their voices are heard or to keep them engaged.

This example applies to other business interactions as well. As mentioned earlier, teleworkers have no water cooler to build informal relationships and no hallway conversations to quickly exchange information. When two employees meet virtually they may not have a large white dry-erase board to brainstorm ideas. However, this is not a roadblock. An informal instant message or blog post may substitute for the chance hallway encounter, providing an opportunity to quickly swap information or news. An online meeting space or even simply e-mailing draft presentations can replace the dry-erase board. It is up to the leader to rethink how to accomplish the same goal while using a different medium.

*Leaders need to rethink how employees can interact in a virtual environment.*

## LEADER ACCELERATOR 19: BUILD A VIRTUAL PRESENCE

"I really struggled when I first started teleworking," John, a two-year teleworking veteran, told us. "I was always rated in the top 10 percent in the past, and then I was ranked just in the middle of the pack. When I finally pressed my boss for what I was doing wrong, she simply told me that I didn't seem too engaged. I didn't understand it. I thought I was always someone people remembered long after the meeting or project was over."

John explained that he usually liked to digest information when he first heard it, carefully analyzing everything that was said or given to him. He usually felt strongest interacting with people one to one and not in group settings. We believe his situation is fairly common. An individual may be a great contributor when physically present but feel lost in the virtual environment. Peers may find the person too quiet on a conference call or ineffective through e-mail communications. The challenge for leaders and teleworking employees is to create a virtual presence, a presence that can be felt wherever the person is located.

"I'm a lot different in conference calls now," John continued. "Sometimes I'll read back what people are saying in my own words to ensure that I understand everything correctly, and to ensure they know I'm actively engaged. Or, even if I truly have nothing of value to add,

I'll simply say something every so often like, 'Hi, this is John. I hear what you're saying, I'm taking it in, and I don't have anything to add at this point.' At least people know I'm still there."

*Leaders and employees need to employ tactics and techniques to make sure others can feel their impact.*

E-mail etiquette can be just as important. John explained, "If an e-mail is addressed to me, and not one of the many I'm courtesy copied on, I make sure I respond. Even if I don't have time to address the specific topic I'll reply back to let the sender know I don't have time at the moment but will respond by a certain time."

A number of simple techniques can be used to build a virtual presence. The point is to make a conscious effort not to let others forget about you among the masses in the cyber realm.

## LEADER ACCELERATOR 20: MEET FACE TO FACE

This leader accelerator may, at first blush, seem out of place. Time and again, though, we found that one of the most potent accelerators in making telework work was to have some physical, face to face interaction. The operative word is "physical."

We understand that a leader doesn't always have the budget or resources to do this. We would also argue that a lot of physical, face to face interaction is not truly necessary. But whenever the opportunity arises, say, at a conference or annual meeting, try to plan a real live face to face meeting with your teleworkers. This fulfills several functions. Most importantly, it provides face time, which is still one of the most recognized variables in the promotion process. Attaching a living, breathing face (not a Web photo) to a voice and e-mail address goes a long way toward embedding an impression.

We've found that in many cases the physical meeting is more helpful as a social interaction than as a specific work-related activity. It is a chance for teleworkers to enjoy some social time with both traditional workers and other teleworkers. This can be in the form of attending a Happy Hour at a local watering hole or just a social dinner. This physical interaction creates stronger and more cohesive bonds and fills in much of what is absent during most of the teleworking year—employees' engaging in true social activities. The personal, outside-work interaction may cement the bond between workers. When e-mail is sent to someone across the country, the sender will see more than an e-mail address. The sender will feel more connected to the person or team, and the recipients will feel more connected to the sender.

*Whenever feasible, get your teleworkers together for a face to face gathering. It'll change the way they telework for the better.*

Again, this is budget dependent. Keep the need for face time in mind during the budget process and look for creative solutions to get your team together at least once a year. It may seem expensive to do, but we think the benefits outweigh the costs many times over.

## LEADER ACCELERATOR 21:
## DON'T MONITOR—RELY ON TRUST

As a teleworking leader, you'll have access to a wide array of monitoring software. If you wish, you'll be able to see and track the e-mail your teleworkers send out, the keystrokes they key in, the Web sites they visit, and the amount of time they are logged in. It may be tempting to go Big Brother on your teleworkers, but we strongly suggest not taking that route. We base this recommendation on several reasons.

Most important, trust is the glue and grease that makes telework work. If you don't trust your workers in the first place, we'd have to wonder why you would agree to a teleworking arrangement. It's precisely because of trust that an offer to telework is extended. Never, never put employees into a telework arrangement if there's a question surrounding their honesty, character, or integrity.

*Don't give in to temptation. Resist monitoring the minute-to-minute activities of your teleworkers. Rely on trust and performance metrics instead.*

Leaders who lead through fear and control are never the best leaders of either traditional workers or teleworkers. There are more professional and acceptable ways to ensure that teleworkers are working. Employing performance metrics and keeping close tabs on performance—not e-mail activity—provides the best window into whether an employee is engaged and productive. Monitoring creates fear and distrust—two forces that collide with the true spirit of telework. Those who lead via a "commitment first" style are much more successful in leading in a virtual world.

# GUIDING PRINCIPLES

Many small factors contribute to a leader's success in implementing and sustaining telework arrangements. To help telework leaders remember all the accelerators that can be used to make telework work, we offer the following as a guide:

*Build a strong foundation.* Set teleworkers up for success by conducting a formal initial counseling, scheduling quarterly counseling sessions, and engaging in informal counseling in between. Formalize the ground rules of the telework arrangement with a written, signed agreement and document the team's mission as well as its basic and core expectations. Develop an exit policy for those who wish to come back to a traditional work assignment. Lastly, don't forget about providing the support and resources for workers to succeed.

*Continually develop teleworkers.* Developing and cultivating teleworkers is just as important as providing a strong foundation and starting things on the right foot. Leaders have several options, such as working with their teleworkers to identify potential personal or technical problems and associated mitigation plans, establishing a mentoring program, or rewarding and publicizing desired teleworking behaviors.

*Don't overlook the importance of building relationships.* Relationships are critically important when it comes to teleworking. Leaders should strive to keep teleworkers visible to the organization by publishing all necessary contact information and finding ways to ensure teleworkers are engaged with others. Different media and technology can also help get the most out of teleworkers. Plan for some physical, face to face interaction whenever possible (at least once a year) to build relationships.

***Create the right technical framework for success.*** Obviously, tele-working relies on technology, but leaders need to keep a couple of things in mind to increase chances for success. First, security should be a top priority—budget both time and money for it. Second, take full advantage of the network and move away from personal storage—make information accessible to all that need it. Lastly, adopt common platforms to ensure information can be shared among all employees.

***Experiment and get personally involved.*** Leaders can experiment with teleworking by investing in a pilot study before rolling out telework technology or new work arrangements. Also, leaders can get personal experience with teleworking before leading teleworkers or virtual teams.

***Build trust.*** Don't waste time trying to micromanage teleworkers' time just to ensure they are working. Implement performance-based metrics that are measured regularly, and build commitment to get the most out of teleworkers. Also, establish consistent standards for both tele-workers and traditional workers to avoid perceptions of hypocrisy and favoritism.

# LEADERSHIP MISTAKES
# AND PITFALLS

*The successful man will profit from his mistakes
and try again in a different way.*
Dale Carnegie

Everyone makes mistakes. Good leaders make bad decisions. Team members fall short of expectations. Projects fail to deliver promised results. And teleworking is no different. From the leaders we spoke with and the organizations we had the opportunity to examine, we saw plenty of examples where teleworking just didn't work. However, to use an old cliché, mistakes can be the stepping stones to success. And this is why we like the quote from Dale Carnegie that opens this chapter. But we would also argue that successful leaders (or organizations, for that matter) don't have to learn from their own mistakes—they can learn from the mistakes or bad experiences of others as well.

Instead of telling you what to do to make telework work, this chapter describes what *not* to do. You may not have all the ingredients to create the perfect teleworking environment, but you can at least steer clear of a variety of traps and pitfalls and thus increase your chances of turning telework into a valuable component of your organization's way of doing business. More important, you can employ tactics and techniques to avoid these pitfalls right now. Let someone else's mistakes be your stepping stones to success.

# LEADERSHIP PITFALL 1:
## NO SPONSORSHIP

Ask any project manager in your organization to tell you the most common reasons of why projects fail. We can almost guarantee that one of the reasons is linked to sponsorship—or rather, the lack of sponsorship. With most projects, a sponsor is a key individual or group within the organization that has a vested interest in the outcome and can provide or align resources for the initiative. The resources provided by the sponsor may come in the form of funding, people, or technology, but they can also be intangible, such as helping to create a vision or establishing direction and communicating it to the rest of the organization.

Obtaining a sponsor in any project is critical. Besides their obvious function of providing the funds necessary to run the project, sponsors help in many ways. The sponsor, usually a high-level leader, is the visible proponent of the effort and can help influence the organization. Sponsors typically have the social capital or status to manage organizational politics or at least ensure that the initiative is not lost among the host of other ongoing, competing efforts. Without sponsorship, it is easy for a project to fall by the wayside. With telework, lack of sponsorship can easily translate to a flailing grassroots effort within the organization.

Revisiting the midsized company that had no takers for its telework program, we were not surprised to find that executive sponsorship was absent.

"How did you decide to launch telework in your company?" we asked an HR analyst.

"Well," he replied, "we did an employee satisfaction survey and knew that many people were upset over their work–life balance, so flextime and telecommuting policies were some of the actions we took."

We were curious. "Who kicked off the initiative?"

"We did. I mean, the president had to approve, but HR made the announcement and launched it."

Immediately, we perceived a problem. "Did the president or any other executive communicate this announcement or reinforce it during company or department meetings?"

"No. The VP of HR talked about it a few times during all-employee meetings and we posted the policies on the company intranet site."

In retrospect, the absence of executive sponsors should have raised red flags in the organization. Without any executive outside HR advocating the new initiative, there was little hope that teleworking could create a foothold in the business. Employees may have perceived a disconnect between the new work arrangements and executive expectations or questioned how serious the business leaders were about making telework work.

"How many people took advantage of the flextime policy or telecommuting?" we asked.

"It's been months since the announcement was made, and to my knowledge, no one has taken us up on either offer."

Even if employee retention is one of the reasons for launching telework, we recommend that sponsors do not come only from Human Resources. Business leaders have to be engaged and on board. To increase chances of success, telework should be driven from the top down. We also suggest finding an executive evangelist—a top-level leader willing to inspire, motivate, and create momentum—to help lead teleworking when it's first introduced. At a minimum, beware of proceeding with telework without adequate sponsorship.

*Ensure you have executive sponsorship before launching telework.*

## LEADERSHIP PITFALL 2:
## NOT GETTING THE MOST OUT OF TELEWORK

Throughout this book we've discussed the many benefits of teleworking, from employee retention to increased productivity to cost savings. However, problems can arise when organizations pursue telework for only one specific benefit. For example, at the company we just described, the HR analyst stated the reason behind teleworking was to create a better work–life balance and increase employee satisfaction. But the focus on employee satisfaction failed to get business leaders to support the initiative or encourage their employees to participate. Telework could never be fully integrated into the business without a more holistic approach.

Any myopic view of telework may prevent telework from taking hold or, worse, lead to negative side effects. For many leaders, telework is attractive because it promises productivity gains or cost savings. With the explosion of mobile devices and wireless technology, workers can work from anywhere at any time. One study found that mobile devices increase employee productivity by just over 13 percent a week.[1] Yet researchers question whether the employees using this technology are becoming more efficient or simply working more hours due to constant connectivity and access to information. Consider that in many traditional work environments employees leave their work behind them when they leave the office for the day. Now, with PDAs, iPhones, and other devices, employees can receive e-mail messages and other communications at the office on the way home, in the evenings, or on the weekends.

"Working from a home office takes a lot of discipline," one former teleworker told us. "I went to work in the morning, worked all day, and in the evening I shut the door of my home office and left for the night—just like I worked in an office building."

Another teleworker admitted the challenges with this kind of self-restraint. He said, "It's hard to just turn off. I work in a different time zone than some of my coworkers. E-mails and messages still come in throughout the day and evening. I can hear my BlackBerry buzzing all night long with new messages. I'm like a moth drawn to the light. I keep checking, responding, and working regardless of the hour."

Even if higher productivity is the only goal for a company's interest in telework, leaders have to be cautious of its implications. Some leaders may rejoice at having instant, constant access to their employees, but in the long run this can destroy employee morale and actually cause decreases in employee output.

The same can be said for telework initiatives that are driven by leaders who only want to reduce their operating expenses. With full-time home-based teleworkers, a company could greatly reduce its physical office needs, lowering its costs. However, this could also reduce satisfaction and productivity for those employees not ready for telework or needing a more structured environment. As a case in point, academic institutions are increasingly drawn to telework in the form of distance-learning classrooms. Universities can save money by conducting classes without the need for physical classrooms or by increasing the number of classes a professor can teach at once. But this approach may limit the interaction between teacher and student or decrease individual student attention—a key contributor to students' choice in selecting where to attend college.

Telework is not intended to be a stand-alone initiative; it should be a value-added component of running a business or organization. Leaders should develop a comprehensive business case to recognize the full benefits of telework. Identifying all the benefits will not only help increase the support and buy-in from stakeholders but will also help create a complete strategy to implement and ensure success.

*Leaders should take a holistic view of telework to maximize its true benefits.*

## LEADERSHIP PITFALL 3: LACK OF PLANNING

Even if the organization has developed a solid business case for why to incorporate telework, more attention must be given to how teleworking will be implemented. The U.S. Army has a good rule of thumb when it comes to planning. Military leaders call it the "one-third, two-thirds rule." Conventional military wisdom states that for every hour a unit is expecting to spend executing, leaders need to spend two hours planning. This ratio expresses the importance of using twice as much time to plan as to execute, and it applies to telework as well.

While with our HR analyst friend, we probed to understand the planning behind the company's implementation.

"After you made your announcement and launched the initiative, what happened?" we asked.

"After we set things in motion, we eventually polled the different teams to see if anyone was using flextime or had started to telecommute," he said.

"Was that it?"

"Pretty much. That's how we knew the new policy didn't have much of an effect."

"Before you made the announcement, what actions did the company take to prepare for the new work arrangements?" we asked.

"Honestly, we left it up to each of the company departments to manage. HR created the policies but the management teams were responsible for managing it."

We were not surprised to learn that the company had not socialized the concept of the new work arrangement with many managers prior to making an announcement to the entire employee population. Also, no training was done and teams had no time to prepare before the launch. Again, the absence of a detailed and documented plan should have raised a red flag.

As we mentioned earlier, implementing telework is similar to any other large-scale project. A myriad of details should be worked out prior to launch. Consider just a few:

- Who will be allowed to telework?

- Will there be a pilot test before the mass rollout?

- How will it be communicated?

- Will training be needed?

- How will teleworkers be supported?

- What contingency plans or exit strategies will be needed?

- How will success be measured and who will do it?

- What are the risks (security, behavior issues, logistics, and the like)?

The list could go on. The answers to these questions could also lead to other follow-up questions or details that need to be addressed. The take-away for leaders is to carefully plan telework. A launch-and-learn approach can quickly devolve into launch-and-burn if leaders fail to consider the many details necessary to make telework work.

After a company makes the commitment to undertake telework, resources should be assigned to plan appropriately. As with other projects, leaders should scope the initiative, for example, deciding who will telework, what parts of a job can be teleworked, and whether the company should conduct a pilot or "full Monty" approach, and they should set the boundaries or expectations for telework. Then, leaders can define what activities are needed to implement the program (communication, training, support, or logistics). Additionally, leaders should consider the potential risks up front and develop action plans to address issues that may rise. The work done in preparation for telework will pay dividends for leaders once it is implemented.

It is important to point out that planning for telework is more about people than about technology. Much attention and money is usually spent on technology, but not enough is devoted to training, education, and developing the interpersonal skills necessary in the telework environment. The technology infrastructure is vital to success, but it is worthless if people do not know how to use it effectively. Too much emphasis on technology not only dehumanizes telework but increases the chance of failure. Leaders must adequately prepare their employees to use the tools needed in the telework environment.

"Tell us about this new collaborative software application we heard about," we asked the HR analyst.

He shrugged his shoulders as if he were embarrassed that we brought it up. He said, "We purchased software that would allow users to share their desktops during meetings. You know, a team could meet over a conference call and everyone could be looking at the same material. One person could share what he was working on in real time and everyone else could see it on their own computer screen. It's like being in the same meeting room working on a big whiteboard."

"That sounds pretty neat."

"It is, except no one really uses it."

"Why's that?" we asked.

"When we implemented our telework plan we mentioned the software in the announcement, but we never trained anyone outside IT how to use it. We identified one subject matter expert, and we told anyone interested to contact her to learn how to use the software. Some people did reach out to her, but for the most part everyone else just went back to what they were used to—e-mail and conference calls."

*Leaders should spend adequate time planning telework before implementing it.*

Changing employee behavior, implementing new technology, training workers, and altering work arrangements—none of these measures are easy. And all of them are involved with telework. Proper planning is essential. Without spending as much time or more on planning than on the actual implementation, leaders may have difficulty getting telework beyond a simple organizational announcement.

## LEADERSHIP PITFALL 4:
## NOT BEING FLEXIBLE

Although we can't overemphasize the importance of developing a detailed plan for telework, leaders must also be able to adapt plans to changes. We hesitate to use the cliché about what happens to the best-laid plans, but it is true to some degree. It is nearly impossible to anticipate all the challenges in implementing telework, and leaders can fall into analysis paralysis if plans are continuously reworked but never executed. The business environment, technology, and the roles people play in the organization continually change. If leaders fail to adapt how they employ telework to new situations then they risk the entire effort. Telework may eventually fail to meet the evolving needs of the business. The best telework leaders we met were like Gumby dolls, flexible and not too rigid.

The telework plan should be frequently reviewed by the executive sponsor and other stakeholders as it is implemented. Progress can be assessed and adjustments or course corrections can be made as needed. Leaders should always be asking *why* if results differ from expectations to uncover the root causes and determine next steps. For example, had the leadership team in the company we've been discussing reviewed the telework implementation a few months after launch and discovered that everyone was still in traditional work arrangements, the team could have delved into the potential reasons. If it was a result of the austere company culture, the leadership team could plan the next steps to influence the culture. Perhaps some of the leaders would lead by example and telework themselves, or they could identify individuals particularly suited to telework and invite them to try it. Once the program had some participants, publicly recognizing teleworkers or their increased productivity would be another option.

Leaders can also use this exercise as an opportunity to identify other areas or applications for telework. Whether the telework implementation is below or above expectations, periodic assessments can ensure that telework is evolving and continually adds value.

*Don't be inflexible! Continually review the plan and make necessary changes.*

# LEADERSHIP PITFALL 5: FORGETTING ABOUT TRADITIONAL WORKERS

It may appear counterintuitive to draw attention to workers in traditional work assignments in a discussion about teleworking. However, unless 100 percent of the organization's employees will be teleworking, traditional office-based workers will be a key component of making telework work. Leaders need to train and educate traditional workers on how to work with their teleworking counterparts.

"This company doesn't know how to deal with virtual workers," one teleworker lamented. Ironically, the company she was working for was a technology manufacturer and prided itself on its teleworking ability.

When we asked for specifics, she said, "One example is the meeting I had this morning. Just over half of the attendees were in the same conference room while the rest of us called in. The people in the room carried on as if those of us on the phone weren't even there. The last company I worked for was much better at including virtual team members. People physically present in a conference wouldn't talk over people on the phone, and meeting organizers would make sure everyone was included in the discussion."

This simple example highlights the need to incorporate traditional workers into the telework training plan. Traditional workers will have to learn new skills to work in the virtual workplace, from handling virtual meetings and the tools necessary to interact with teleworkers to basic communication skills. Without nonverbal cues such as facial expressions and body language, both teleworkers and traditional types will have to sharpen their ability to communicate via the phone, e-mail, instant messaging, or other online tools. The obvious friction that can occur between traditional workers and teleworkers can be avoided if leaders give equal attention to both groups while realizing the different needs of each.

*Don't forget about traditional workers—they will need to be trained and educated as well.*

# LEADERSHIP PITFALL 6:
# MEASURING THE WRONG THINGS

If you want to avoid the pitfall of micromanaging teleworkers, how can you ensure that teleworkers are productive? Beyond establishing a leadership foundation based on commitment and trust, we recommend implementing performance-based metrics. Nonetheless, another pitfall lurks in this concept. "What gets measured gets done," as the saying goes—and it's especially true for telework.

When we asked one manager how she knew if her teleworkers were productive, she replied, "I check their instant message status."

We asked for her to elaborate. She said, "It's easy. On the company's instant message system I can tell if they're logged in to the network. If their laptop is inactive for a couple of minutes, then the instant message application automatically shows that they're away. Basically, I can tell when they log on and log off for the day, and if they're active."

We cringed at the thought of our instant message status being monitored, but it seems like a simple idea. The leader has a virtual way to see when her employees come to work, take breaks, or shut down for the day. Yet it would be just as easy for an employee to get around this. The application settings can be set to show it as always active or left on. The resulting impression would be no different from that made by an in-house employee who hangs around and leaves only after the boss has left the building first. More important, it doesn't measure productivity or performance. In fact, the measurement may be counterproductive and encourage undesired behavior. By developing a metric likely to be perceived as an exercise in micromanagement, the leader may destroy any bond of trust with employees, decrease team morale, and ultimately lower team performance.

Another teleworker told us, "It's harder to put one over on the boss. In the old days, you could hang around the water cooler, or at least be in the office at your desk, and you could look productive. With teleworking you just can't create that type of show."

We believe this comment is only true if the leader has the right metrics in place. For example, if the leader measures productivity by the teleworker's e-mail volume, then it would not be difficult to churn out lots of worthless messages. In the age where PowerPoint presentations dominate company environments, it's not hard to create visually stunning slide decks that have little substance. Leaders have to be careful in choosing the metrics to measure performance. People will always find a way to meet the measures they are held to, so it's the leader's responsibility to select metrics that drive the right employee behaviors. Choosing the right metric is just as important as selecting target performance levels, or more so.

Leaders should prefer a combination of lagging and leading metrics. *Lagging metrics* refer to the desired outcomes and are typically easy to develop. For example, lagging indicators may refer to project deliverables or quarterly financial goals. *Leading indicators* are the predictors of the desired outcomes and may reflect the behaviors needed to meet the lagging indicator targets. For example, an account manager may have a fiscal-year goal of revenue per region (lagging indicator) with

*Pick the right metrics! A combination of lagging and leading metrics is more effective than either type alone.*

additional goals around new customers identified or number of contracts renewed (leading indicators). Using both lagging and leading indicators should provide a healthy balance for the leader to ensure teleworkers will meet expectations.

## LEADERSHIP PITFALL 7: BECOMING "MISSING IN ACTION"

Although micromanaging teleworkers is apt to be counterproductive, the opposite extreme is not a favorable alternative. It is important for the leader not to be completely absent or too hands-off. Leaders who are missing in action can leave teleworkers feeling alienated or downright abandoned.

According to one survey of five hundred workers, approximately half responded that their jobs would be more difficult if they didn't work in the same office location as their boss. A quarter stated that it made their job much more difficult. Ironically, less than 15 percent of executive respondents in the same survey felt it was important to be in the same office location as their staff.[2] The survey results tell an interesting story. Apparently, leaders may be more comfortable with the idea of teleworking or remote working than their employees. We expect that employees will eventually shift their attitudes to align with the executives surveyed, given the increasing trend toward telework arrangements. However, for now, leaders will have to contend with employees who feel discomfort when physically disconnected from their managers. It is the leader's responsibility to keep the virtual office door open and maintain strong ties with the employees.

A leader has many techniques to employ to stay connected even when face to face interaction is not possible. Although a predominant amount of business is done via e-mail, leaders can use the oldest form of teleworking, the telephone. Individual phone conversations and conference calls are recommended in many cases over e-mail to create more personal relationships. Webcams are relatively inexpensive and can make phone calls more expressive by attaching a face to a voice. One step up from webcams are telepresence technologies, such as the equipment created by Cisco, Hewlett-Packard, or Polycom. Telepresence employs large high-definition screens with superior sound to allow users to feel as if they were actually present. Telepresence technologies do not have the latency issues or low resolution of webcams and can make workers feel more connected. However, commonly available technologies, such as instant messaging applications or simple procedures such as e-mailed status reports that highlight various activities, can also be used effectively. Regardless of the specific technique, the leader should recognize the existence of a multitude of methods to create interactions with teleworkers.

*Don't be too hands-off! Leaders need to use available technology to connect with teleworkers.*

## LEADERSHIP PITFALL 8: BEING TOO QUICK TO PULL THE PLUG ON TELEWORK

Blogs and online discussion forums buzzed in 2006 when AT&T recalled an unreported number of its five thousand teleworkers. The move was surprising considering that AT&T was an early adopter of telecommuting, starting in 1992. Three years later, thirty-five thousand managers were telecommuting at least one day a week.[3] The company affirmed its support for telecommuting and telework but claimed the move was to consolidate operations and merge with assets of BellSouth, Cingular, and SBC. Still, many wondered how it might affect other companies planning to implement telework to see a pioneer reel in some of its workers, regardless of the reason behind the move.

Unfortunately, AT&T was not alone. During the same period, Hewlett-Packard recalled an unspecified number of teleworkers—a surprising move from the company that invented flexible work arrangements. Computer chip manufacturer Intel also recalled some of its teleworking IT personnel. And the federal government reported a telework drop of over 7 percent from 2005 to 2006.

We are not arguing against the moves of AT&T, HP, Intel, or the federal government. AT&T went through several mergers and acquisitions. HP's decision seemed to be part of a number of changes introduced by a new chief executive to consolidate operations. The federal government's actions were based on growing security concerns. However, we offer a warning to leaders who implement telework and then at some point try to reduce or remove it. The negative perception created by such a decision, despite the legitimate business reason to do so, can have repercussions for all employees.

Employees who have experienced the benefits of teleworking, whether they think of the increased productivity, better work–life balance, or reduced stress due to lack of commute, may be reluctant to go back to traditional work assignments. Online posts, supposedly from AT&T employees, did not view the move as favorable. Some employees claimed that they would leave the company. Other posts from teleworkers outside the company also stated that they would leave their current employer if told to abandon their telework arrangement. A decision to scale back teleworking can potentially drive away talent or at least drive down the morale of teleworkers, and it can impact all employees as well. Pulling back may be viewed as a failure and discourage future efforts to integrate teleworking. Worse, employees may view the decision as a broken promise. If company management were to renege on one agreement with employees, would it do so on obligations such as compensation, benefits, or other employee programs?

We've mentioned that leaders should have an exit strategy for individual teleworkers, but we strongly caution against a mass exit. Leaders have several options to avert this pitfall. Before launching telework, a pilot program with a select number of employees could validate the business case and help identify issues prior to a company-wide, or department-wide, rollout. Leaders should also assess the amount of teleworking to incorporate into the business or organizational operations. For example, is the plan to let workers operate remotely or to institute flexible work arrangements to allow employees the option to work from home part of the week or part of the workday?

Lastly, leaders should also determine potential elements of an employee's job that can be teleworked. In the future work environment, there may be few employees strictly working in what we would classify as a traditional role—spending eight hours a day in an actual office and working with other employees through face to face meetings. When we spoke with office-bound workers at one large West Coast company, we were surprised at their reliance on telework technology, from webcams to online collaboration tools to simple conference calls.

"Why do you need this technology if you are all here in the same location?" we asked one program manager.

She laughed. "Have you had a tour of the location yet? Do you know how many dozens of buildings are on this campus? There's no way I could spend my entire day bouncing back and forth between buildings trying to meet everyone in person when I could spend that time actually getting work done."

Even if workers need to be in an office location, telework technology can still be used to increase productivity and may be more efficient in some cases than physical interactions. Telework presents leaders with interesting opportunities to best use technology to get work done. Putting a heavy amount of effort in planning for the telework implementation, coupled with experimentation and thought around how the technologies can be best used, can help make it unnecessary to roll back telework after it is introduced.

*Be cautious of scaling back telework after it's introduced.*

# LEADERSHIP PITFALL 9:
# INFORMATION OVERLOAD

Try to imagine running your business without e-mail. Everyone has become so dependent on this technology that it is hard to remember what people did before its inception. The problem today is that we have too much of it. With mobile communications such as PDAs, people can receive information 24/7. Our inboxes reach maximum capacity and BlackBerrys turn into "Crack-Berrys" as we continually try to keep up with the incoming volume. In an internal study conducted by Intel, the company discovered that knowledge workers, those working primarily with information, spend up to twenty hours a week just reading and responding to e-mail.[4] Furthermore, the study found that approximately one-third of the e-mails were worthless. Six hours a week, almost a full workday, was wasted on ineffective e-mail communications.

And it's not just e-mail. Instant messaging applications can be invasive and disruptive, too.

"I used to love IM," one director told us. "It's great to be able to get hold of someone immediately, whether they're at home or even in another meeting. In many cases, I can get hold of someone faster through IM than calling them on the phone. But I get so many instant messages through the day that it gets me off track. I barely get fifteen minutes of work done before someone is pinging me and fighting for my attention."

Today, we have more access to data and information than ever before. Business intelligence applications are in increasing demand as corporate teams try to synthesize all the data their systems can collect. Individual users do not have to rely on corporate channels for information when they can easily go to countless sources on the Internet.

More is not always better. More communication does not translate into more effective communication. Information overload can cause cognitive disruption—an inability to focus on the task at hand. As leaders and workers receive a constant barrage of information, many divert their attention to handle each issue or problem put in front of them.

This results in a LIFO (last-in, first-out) system of working through a worker's electronic inbox. This hampers productivity because it eliminates prioritization of tasks. Additionally, it can interfere with strategic thinking as well. Leaders can spend nearly all of their attention on the immediate tasks that pop up and have little time to focus on long-term issues. Imagine flying an airplane and viewing the instruments in the cockpit when every light is flashing and alarm buzzing. Where do you focus your attention?

Information overload is of particular concern to teleworkers. Teleworkers rely on communication technologies such as e-mail and instant messaging. Leaders need to avoid the trap of letting their teleworkers get bogged down and should emphasize *effective communications* rather than the *volume* of communications. E-mail communications should be short and to the point. Recipients should be able to understand the content in only a minute. E-mail users may need to be retrained on not filling up the "cc" line or clicking "Reply All" when it is not necessary. Planned e-mail or IM "quiet times" are also a good idea to allow team members to block times for uninterrupted activities.

Information overload can also lead to poor decision making due to the shortened time workers spend reviewing their messages and the potential conflict of information between data sources. Teleworkers rely on access to various information sources to get their job done. Unfortunately, information can differ on specific points based on numerous issues such as the type of data collected, when data is collected or loaded, or how business rules are applied to interpreting data. Entire industries have evolved over data management and business intelligence to ensure that leaders and employees have the right information necessary to make decisions. We are not suggesting that every leader has to be an expert on data management, but leaders do have a responsibility to help their teleworkers identify commonly accepted sources of information and avoid conflicts. Relying on inaccurate, incomplete, or questionable information can cause a breakdown in communications between team members, lower morale, and reduce productivity.

*Don't let teleworkers become crushed by information overload. Strive for effective communication rather than high-volume communication.*

# LEADERSHIP PITFALL 10:
## SECURITY, PART 2

In Chapter 6 we highlighted the importance of security, and the subject is important enough to mention again. Lack of information security can be the death of teleworking or at least a legitimate reason to restrict it from reaching its full potential. The recall of federal government teleworkers over security concerns is a case in point.

One study (involving more than two thousand remote workers from various industries and company sizes in ten countries) revealed that remote workers engage in risky online behavior.[7] Although respondents generally agreed that working remotely involved security risks, their behaviors did not align to this sentiment. The risky behavior ranged from opening e-mails from suspicious sources to hijacking wireless connections from neighbors to accessing company files with nonprotected devices.

Even more disturbing is the finding that remote workers loaned work computers to nonemployees and the prevailing perception that Internet usage was safe as long as they were not connected to the company network. With the line between an employee's professional and personal life becoming increasingly blurry, many companies allow, or at least accept, some degree of personal use of work computers. However, many users are unaware of the hazards they face even if they are not connected to the company's network. *Malware,* malicious software such as worms, spyware, Trojan horses, or Web robots, can be attached when browsing the Internet and later be introduced to the company network when the user logs in.

*Make security a top priority! Make sure teleworkers understand the risks poor behavior poses to the company.*

Leaders should start by educating their teleworkers on organization policies regarding Internet and computer usage. Teleworkers should also have an understanding of the potential threats and impacts to the organization. As reinforcement, training should be done at regular intervals and not as a one-time event. Additionally, leaders should work with their IT departments to understand the technologies in place that can help deal with security risks or reduce the likelihood of actual harm.

## LEADERSHIP PITFALL 11:
## ASSUMING SUCCESS TRANSLATES EVERYWHERE

It is important to note that since every organization is different, approaches to telework will have to vary slightly based on the type of work done, organizational culture, maturity of the organization, employee experience, and so on. It is dangerous to attempt a cookie-cutter approach and apply teleworking exactly as it is done in another organization or even another department or team within the same organization. We still advocate benchmarking and adopting best practices wherever leaders find them, but we are recommending that leaders identify the distinct needs and differences of their own teams to understand how to best to make telework work.

Applying a telework plan that does not exactly fit the team's needs may cause loss of momentum for telework as the teleworkers struggle to develop workaround solutions for problems unique to their team. For example, the company's sales team may be a mobile workforce, working from home offices and predominantly on the road. Their team structure naturally lends itself to telework since they are scattered across customer locations. Their working needs may be based on receiving real-time data such as price quotes or order status. The culture supports telework since many are traveling almost full-time and do not regularly meet with their supervisors face to face. This is different from the operations team in the same company, which is implementing a flexible work arrangement in which employees can work from home several days a week. The business analysts have different needs, usually reviewing large amounts of data that could take days to assemble and presenting reports of this data analysis to upper management. Furthermore, the workers in operations may be used to physical interactions on a daily basis. Although the operations team can learn a lot from the sales group in terms of teleworking, not all the lessons will apply.

*Leaders should benchmark and collect best practices before implementation, but should also understand which provisions apply to a particular context or situation and which do not.*

If the operations leader attempts to implement telework exactly like that of the sales department, the team could run into a variety of problems. The business analysts could feel disaffected at the sudden loss of physical contact with peers and supervisors. They may also require additional training on how to telework effectively, and they may need different support in order to accomplish their daily tasks. Leaders should collect best practices from other teleworking groups but also understand the specific needs of each particular group and how teleworking is used to meet those requirements. Leaders can then identify the needs of their own area and perform a gap analysis to identify which ideas are likely to work and which ideas will need to be modified.

# GUIDING PRINCIPLES

Telework leaders have to recognize and be aware of the many dangers associated with teleworking. Here are some common telework pitfalls:

*Beware of implementing without leadership involvement.* Before launching telework, leaders should start off by obtaining an executive sponsor. Sponsors can help remove roadblocks and provide momentum. Leaders should also work with sponsors to develop a holistic strategy that will make sure telework is integrated into the business.

*Plan, plan, plan—but don't forget to remain flexible.* Leaders should count on spending twice as much time planning for telework as on its implementation. Planning for telework is similar to any other large-scale project. Activities, risks, dependencies, and resources should be identified before launch. However, not all changes or challenges can be anticipated. Periodically review the telework plan, address issues, and make necessary modifications.

*Be careful of retracting telework.* Beware of scaling back or recalling teleworkers after the program is introduced. Don't be too quick to squeeze the trigger. Teleworkers may be reluctant to go back to traditional work assignments. Piloting before full implementation and being selective of what jobs or parts of jobs can be teleworked can reduce the risk of a mass exit.

# GUIDING PRINCIPLES cont.

***Don't disengage with traditional workers (or with teleworkers).*** Leaders should not lose sight of either traditional workers or teleworkers; each group will have its own special needs. Traditional workers will require attention in the form of education and training to help them acquire new skills to work with teleworkers and virtual teams. Leaders who do not engage often with teleworkers can leave teleworkers feeling alienated. There are a number of methods and technologies to ensure the leader stays connected to the team.

***Be smart about how you measure performance.*** Leaders should implement a healthy balance of leading and lagging performance-based metrics. Careful consideration of a small set of selected metrics will help prevent undesired behaviors. Although benchmarking is helpful, leaders should also recognize the different needs of their own group and what practices or metrics may not apply or may need to be modified.

***Don't let teleworkers suffer from information overload.*** The flood of information from electronic sources can weigh down teleworkers and make them less effective. Focus on quality rather than quantity of communications, data, or metrics.

***Don't ignore security risks.*** Security has to be a primary concern for leaders. Continually review company policies and practices with teleworkers to ensure good (and safe) working habits. Partner with the IT department to implement technology to minimize potential risks.

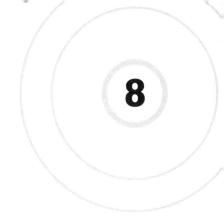

# THE FUTURE WORK ENVIRONMENT

*The future is always beginning now.*
**Mark Strand**

Predicting the future is always a dangerous game. The future is fickle; it changes and takes unexpected turns. Going by mid-twentieth-century prognostications, everyone should now be flying around in jetpacks, vacationing on the moon, and eating a full three-course meal in a pill the size of a Tylenol—and not dealing with the Internet and the far-reaching implications of the Web. It is equally likely that unforeseeable explosions of technology and innovation in the coming years will change life in and out of organizations in unimaginable ways. However, at the risk of embarrassing ourselves, we offer our own list of possibilities. Examining some current trends, we look to the near future and grapple with their potential implications for teleworkers, leaders, organizations, and, even, societies.

## THE CHANGING WORKFORCE AND
## THE WORK–LIFE IMBALANCE

The workforce in the United States is changing dramatically. The Millennial generation, the workers about to flood organizations, will force organizations to change their thinking on how to compensate and interact with their employees. The Millennials, Generation Y, are a re-markable bunch: They've never known a VCR player, the Internet has always existed, and paper maps are foreign. Millennials are quick to forge relationships through personal connections made without ever physically shaking the hand of the person they bond with. The success of social networking sites such as MySpace, Facebook, and countless others highlights their comfort with online relationship building. Pre-Internet generations may complain and resist the idea of working re-motely without the ability to physically meet with their peers, share the same meeting room with employees, or get face time with bosses, but Millennial workers require less in this regard. Their personal devel-opment coincided with the maturation of the Internet, and the result is a workforce that readily accepts telework.

Millennials also have different expectations about work–life bal-ance from those of their Baby Boomer (Generation X) parents. Grow-ing up, Millennials may have watched both parents work sixty hours a week or more. They may remember the recession in the 1990s or the dot-com bust in the beginning of this century. They have witnessed the rise of outsourcing and offshoring, and they have watched the debacles of Enron, WorldCom, and others. Millennials have little trust in large corporations. *What's in it for me?* they ask. Work–life balance is a prior-ity, even over compensation for some. They regard flextime, or other programs that reduce the rigidity of work hours and make it possible for them to not only work hard but enjoy life away from work, as a necessity.

This is not to say that older workers do not want the same balance in their life. As workers near retirement they too desire flexibility, more time to spend with family, and even the opportunity to work remotely. The opportunity here appears counterintuitive. Both the early (Millen-nial) and the late (Boomer) generations will be looking for organiza-tions that offer flexibility and creative work designs.

However, despite the desire of all of these workers to reduce work-ing hours and increase personal time, people will be working more, not less. The prevalence of more powerful mobile devices, the expansion of wireless connectivity, and the increased storage of information on com-pany networks (instead of on personal devices) translate into one sim-ple fact: You will always be connected. Already, most workers always have access to their organization, and their organization always has access to them. Throughout this book, we have argued the benefits of connectivity and the ability to work without boundaries of physical presence. We would be remiss if we did not highlight the challenges. We suspect a growing tension as the line between work life and personal life blurs and eventually fades away completely. The desire for work–life balance may increase, but the reality will remain more elusive.

Leaders need to recognize the gap between worker expectations and the reality of the job. Restraint will need to be exercised in some cases. Simply, just because the leader always has access to the employees doesn't mean the leader should use it. Leaders may even have to enforce some separation, such as encouraging vacation time or "e-mail blackout days," to avoid overworking or burning out employees. You may be thinking that individual employees are responsible

> **Both incoming and outgoing generations will demand a better work–life balance—the leader can help them achieve it.**

for managing their own time and unplugging themselves from the organization when necessary. We agree, in part. Employees do have a responsibility to strike their own balance, but the behavior and actions of their leaders set the foundation. Leaders can help increase employee satisfaction (and employee productivity) by not giving in to the temptation of abusing the instant, constant access to their employees.

## The Shifting Population

It is interesting to speculate that, if taken to the extreme, teleworking could impact shifts in regional population. If an employee is not physically tied to a company location and can truly work from anywhere, why not relocate to a more suitable or enjoyable spot? Why would anyone who disliked snow live in upstate New York? Why not move to Arizona or Florida? On a mass scale, could popular spots in the coastal Southeast or the economically affordable locales in the Southwest see their populations rise? Will certain towns or cities become teleworking hubs to attract future teleworkers?

Historically, the working population has moved or settled down based on where an organization needed them. However, over the next several decades the choice of where to live could lie completely within the realm of the employee. Employees could relocate based on personal preferences such as climate or cost of living. From a civic policy perspective, massive migrations could have severe impacts on local economies. The population of locations that are not desirable, for whatever reason, could decline rapidly. Future policymakers could face severe challenges as the tax base for their area quickly erodes. Local businesses would feel the pain as their customer base leaves the area. Housing markets would also be hit hard as the demand for homes in these areas receded. Policymakers may struggle to provide the same quality of life to the citizens left behind.

*Teleworking results in flexibility for the employee and the organization—but it is up to the leader to determine the parameters.*

Large-scale migrations could have sociological implications as well. With work-related relocations, it is hard for families to stay together— even the nuclear family (a concept framed in the era of post–World War II industrialization to distinguish the unit formed by parents and their children from the broader extended family) sometimes struggles with the problem. In a teleworking future, the extended family could be reborn as teleworkers have the option of moving close to relatives of their own or earlier generations.

During the course of our research we spoke with a number of teleworkers who had already relocated based on a variety of personal reasons. Three employees working for a company based on the West Coast each had recently moved—one to Utah, one to Oregon, and the other to Hawaii. All reported a smooth transition to off-site locations with no loss in productivity and much higher satisfaction with their current living conditions. (Did we mention that one moved to Hawaii?) All three moves were made at the employee's expense and with their manager's approval.

"My manager was completely open to the move," the Oregon-based employee said. "I was anxious for a personal change and approached my manager with the idea. He only stipulated that I live in the same time zone."

Interestingly, the other newly relocated employees did not face the same time zone requirements. Leaders will ultimately need to decide if employee-preferred moves are acceptable and what considerations will need to be taken into account. For example, will the employee need to physically meet with others, and if so, does the relocation add additional travel costs? Is the relocation paid by the employee or by the organization, or both? Does the move cross time zones and require additional agreements between the employee and supervisor, such as working hours or availability? Teleworking opens the door for employees to work from anywhere, but leaders will have to weigh the benefits (such as higher productivity or increased retention) with the costs of each chosen location.

## COMPETING IN THE GLOBAL TALENT POOL

These days, the world is flat. As author Thomas Friedman pointed out, the advances in communication technology have created an interconnected world that allows less industrialized nations to compete. Teleworking makes it easier for a worker in Omaha to compete with the local talent in Atlanta for a job in a Georgia-based company. Now, the playing field is leveled on a global scale. The résumé from the Omaha teleworker may sit in a stack of virtual résumés from Bangalore, Shanghai, or Sâo Paulo. It's a scary thought for some U.S. workers: The technology that connects us and makes telework work has now introduced a few billion people into the effective talent pool for U.S. jobs.

Early in the book, we mentioned the success of teleteaching, how universities and schools can apply teleworking to teaching. Some universities now have a model that is almost completely reliant on teleteaching. The school benefits by lowering overhead costs and developing the capacity to reach more students than in a physical classroom. Students benefit from the flexibility of taking online classes and the ability to obtain a higher education that might not be possible near their homes. It can be a win–win relationship for the school and the student. But now take the concept one step further: Why should the school administration pay a local PhD when it can pay a lower rate for an instructor with the same level of education living in Nigeria or Budapest? Some may scoff at this idea, but technology is making the issue a reality.

For years, we witnessed the steady outsourcing and offshoring of jobs to places in Mexico, India, China, or Southeast Asia. It started with manufacturing jobs but quickly caught on for services as firms realized they could ship repetitive processes such as data entry or data processing to low-cost countries. As time passed, the complexity of the work performed by these offshore outsource vendors grew, and they began to offer customer service, data analysis, and other services. In the future, it may be hard to distinguish between the work offered by knowledge workers in another country and by workers in our own. A simple analogy can help explain the challenges of working in a global economy where knowledge becomes almost a commodity.

---

### WORKING WITH NO BARRIERS

A close friend of ours, Linda, opened an online business reselling children's clothing. The beauty of the Internet is that anyone can be an online entrepreneur. With start-up costs low, Linda found it easy to launch her Web site and open her virtual doors for business. However, the site generated numerous hits but few sales. Linda was confused. She had done her homework, researched her market, tested that market before investing in inventory, and followed up with customers. As months went by with little upturn in sales, Linda was faced with a decision of making a large personal investment in salvaging the online store or just cutting her losses by shutting down the business. Linda struggled to understand why her business, which had seemed such a good idea, was not taking off.

Harvard business professor Michael Porter outlined in the late 1970s the forces that determine the competitiveness or attractiveness of a market. The threat of new market entrants, the threat of substitute products, the bargaining power of suppliers or customers, and the intensity of competitive rivalry can all help predict the success of new enterprises. In Linda's case, her biggest challenges was the absence of barriers to entry for competitors. Anyone could set up a similar Web site and offer the same product or service. Furthermore, customers faced no switching costs for choosing another site over hers. Clearly, Linda had entered a difficult market and didn't realize it.

Future teleworkers could face challenges with the potential explosion of workers into the global talent pool. With minimal entry barriers in the labor market, individual teleworkers may find the future playing field much tougher than today's. Employers may have many candidates to choose from and could find many substitutes for any given selected candidate. Education, certification, or basic skills may not be enough to distinguish one candidate from the rest of the pack.

"I can't believe I'm in my late forties and still find myself having to learn new tools, skills, and ways of doing business," one experienced teleworker told us. *Get used to it,* we thought. Future teleworkers, and telework leaders, will need to continually learn new skills and seek self-development just to stay competitive.

*Competing in the global talent pool will require teleworkers and leaders to continually learn new skills and seek self-development opportunities.*

A clear message for policymakers is the need to focus on our educational system. Ultimately, the United States will have to produce better, more educated workers along the entire spectrum of work from manufacturing to specialty to trade to highly skilled, complex occupations. If U.S. workers are to remain competitive on a global scale, then creating an educated, skilled workforce will have to be a top priority. The future of our teleworkforce depends on it.

## Bring in the Hired Guns

In the course of our research, we noticed that in many companies, headcount numbers were scrutinized and management chose to keep headcount numbers low by augmenting the staff with contractors. These independent contractors were typically paid a higher rate than their full-time peers, but the company saved money by not having to pay the fully loaded costs associated with regular employees, such as benefits. In many cases, organizations seemed to skirt the legal boundary between regular employees and contractors. Contractors were hired for a specific purpose and for limited time periods, but often stayed with the company working in different capacities or on new programs or projects.

We couldn't help but wonder if there was a future intersection between contractors and teleworkers. In geographically constrained markets, employers are forced to grow their own talent. With access to global talent pools, employers will have more alternatives. Some employers may not feel the need to develop their employees when it's easy to find a new employee with a desired skill set. The emotional switching costs of replacing employees may be lower due to the lack of physical proximity, and the financial switching costs are also reduced without the need to physically relocate new personnel. Organizations could turn to teleworking contractors with specialized skills for short-term gains, hiring contractors for limited periods to complete specific assignments rather than cultivating employees for a long-term career.

We believe that the best organizations will not simply rely on contractors to fill the ranks of the workforce. Successful organizations will still need to build an internal talent pool and develop people able to lead the organization in the future. However, we do believe that the proportion of contractors in the organizational ranks is very likely to continue to rise. The challenge is not just for teleworkers but for leaders as well. Someone still has to manage and lead workers regardless of their employment status. Many managers we met admitted it was easier at times to manage contractors, but still the leader is leading people and not simply programming automatons. Leaders will have to be flexible and comfortable with the high turnover. Succession planning could be a key management skill as leaders try to maintain continuity between incoming and outgoing personnel. Successful leaders will have to be able to forge relationships quickly and build teams despite the constant flux of new personnel. Additionally, leaders will have to be creative in shortening the learning curve and more quickly socializing new workers.

*Future leaders may have to learn to build relationships and teams quickly amid high turnover.*

## The Global Mind-set

Whether or not the spread of teleworking causes an increase in contracting compared to traditional employment arrangements, we are fairly certain of one eventuality: tomorrow's leaders will need a global mind-set. Organizations are increasingly becoming more global in their reach and in terms of their workforce. Leaders are now more likely to have teams that are increasingly diverse in terms of culture or nationalities. And these teams are apt to be very diverse in their needs, desires, motivation, and attitudes, and in their preferred verbal and nonverbal communication styles.

### LANGUAGE BARRIERS IN THE SAME LANGUAGE

One almost comical story we learned involves the merger of U.S. and British supply companies. It was easy to take for granted that both sides spoke the same language, but leaders soon found that Queen's English and U.S. English were far apart at times, especially when it came to using common terms or idioms. When U.S. managers briefed their new British directors, the directors often responded to every new proposal by saying "Brilliant." Although the British only meant "that's interesting" when they used the word, the U.S. side heard it as validation of their ideas and permission to move forward.[1] One can only picture a conference call between the two sides with nothing to go on but the actual syntax used and no other method to interpret the needs or desires of the other party.

To be effective, leaders will have to be adept at quickly learning and understanding the various backgrounds and cultures of the people that make up their teams. This includes but goes far beyond their languages and customs. Building relationships through media such as e-mail, conference calls, instant messaging, and other methods will be vital. The spatial separation between leaders and team members will force leaders to be even more aware of written and verbal communications. Leaders will need to have a heightened sensitivity, especially a greater cultural sensitivity, when it comes to sensing

*Learning to adapt work styles to create cohesive teams consisting of members from around the world will be critical for future leaders.*

conflict or misunderstanding. Thorough and repetitive follow-up may be required to make sure tasks, messages, or intent are understood by all. Ultimately, the leader's responsibility will be to creatively work through challenges and modify traditional practices to create a cohesive, high-performing team.

## WEB 2.0

*Web 2.0* is a term used primarily to describe the collection of technologies that allows users to share information online and collaborate more effectively. The first generation of the Internet, or Web 1.0, can be thought of as a way to provide content for users, while Web 2.0 is more participatory, allowing users to create the content. Think of a standard Web site compared to the various newer technologies such as blogs, wikis, and social networking sites. In traditional Web sites, users can only view information provided by the site owner, but with a wiki, users actually control the information. This technology is disruptive in the sense that it changes the way people communicate from top-down to mass collaboration.

Throughout this book we have mentioned several of the Web 2.0 technologies and their potential value to leaders and teleworkers. The technology allows for mass collaboration without the need for physical contact between those supplying or using information. Web 2.0 creates a level playing field for teleworking employees. It is a true virtual environment where everyone is connected regardless of location.

Mass collaboration will be a huge benefit to organizations by harnessing the collective knowledge of everyone inside and even those outside the organization. An early adopter of this practice was a Canadian gold mining company that was having trouble locating gold on its properties. In an unprecedented move, it published all of its formerly confidential geological data on the Web and turned the search into a contest, allowing outside users to apply their own skills to help identify new gold deposits. Supposedly, for a half million dollars in prize money, the company was able to identify deposits resulting in billions of dollars of new revenue.[2]

Other companies are starting to use the same approach to solve problems, gather new ideas, identify new markets, or improve products.

A whole movement has organized around the "open-source" computer operating system called Linux. Developers and programmers have contributed knowledge and ideas to create an operating system that rivals any commercial software. The underlying source code can be freely used, passed along, or changed by anyone, and several companies have found it possible to sell *distributions*—packages made up of Linux itself and related utilities—without changing the basic openness of the system. Similarly, we've already mentioned earlier the approach used by Microsoft and its Most Valued Professional award. By encouraging outside users to participate in online forums to discuss the company's products, Microsoft is able to identify bugs with its applications or improve on its products.

Many organizations are starting to use social networking sites to tap into their entire employee base. What started out as popular, personal networking with the Generation Y crowd is now being applied to business and operations. Facebook and MySpace gained popularity to link people with similar interests, but organizations can now use the same technology to identify their own people with critical skills or specific subject matter expertise. And those individuals can now freely contribute on their own to problems, projects, or subject-matter discussions outside their normal, defined area of responsibility. For example, the federal government has an internal wiki that brings together thousands of people from various intelligence agencies. These officials can easily communicate across agency boundaries, once a difficult task for the policy-laden bureaucracies.[3]

Despite the numerous benefits, the use of Web 2.0 technology presents some interesting leadership challenges. First, the explosion of collaboration can leave some employees alienated as they struggle to differentiate their contributions and establish their personal value to the organization. Second, leaders in the future will be bombarded by more and more information. Leaders will be required to quickly interpret, process, and validate useful information—and

*Web 2.0 technologies create an opportunity for teleworkers to contribute as much as any worker in a traditional work assignment.*

separate it from what is not. Lastly, the inevitable introduction of new technology will require leaders to identify its uses in their environments and seize opportunities before their competitors do so.

## Who Benefits from Collaboration?

Organizations clearly benefit from the increased collaboration and availability of information, but it can be much harder to see what's in it for the individuals who contribute their knowledge. For teleworkers, these Web 2.0 technologies give individual employees more opportunity to contribute without any need for physical interaction. However, because everyone shares knowledge in the Web 2.0 environment, individuals may feel that the knowledge that once made them valuable to the organization is now a commodity. The expertise or experience held by any individual is now shared with everyone. Imagine an internal company social networking site where employees can contribute to a wide range of problems or projects. What if outsiders are included in this social networking site? Would some internal employees feel threatened that external people are providing more added value than they are? In the gold mining company mentioned earlier, why would the company need a staff of geologists if outsiders are offering more, and even better, information?

The implication for workers, both traditional workers and teleworkers, is that they will have to provide more than just subject matter expertise. In the future, workers will have to demonstrate their ability to *use* information and not just supply it. Workers will have to quickly build on the ideas of others or use the information provided to take them in new directions. In this manner, workers can benefit too. Think of the open-source code that Linux provides. A programmer creates code openly for others to view, change, and use. Others will help refine or improve the original work of the programmer. The programmer can then use this information to develop more code or solve other problems, leaping ahead faster than would be possible alone. Workers benefit in much the same way organizations do. Through mass collaboration, workers can ultimately deliver and do more.

*Mass collaboration will benefit both organizations and individuals. Better results can be achieved faster through the application of collective knowledge.*

Web 2.0 technologies also have implications for leaders. Leaders who tend toward traditional command-and-control structures will have difficulty adapting to the variety of new technologies that encourage employees to work outside established boundaries. Workers will be likely to collaborate with people outside their team, their department, or even their organization. Leaders who desire to know or keep tabs on everything their employees are doing will find it impossible to keep up.

*Future leaders will need to empower their employees and provide autonomy to deliver the best results.*

If direct control is not an option, then the solution for future leaders is to rely on empowerment rather than control. Measuring employees against performance-based metrics and on deliverables instead of activities will be the only way for leaders to evaluate their workers. Developing relationships founded in trust and commitment and then providing workers autonomy to create, experiment—and even fail—will be a necessity.

## The Leader as Synthesizer

In the age of the Internet and access to instantaneous information, the newspaper industry seems doomed. Who wants to trudge down to the end of the driveway wearing a bathrobe and a slicker in the middle of a morning thunderstorm for day-old information when up-to-the-minute news is available at a mouse-click? Newspapers are losing readership. Classifieds and advertisements used to generate significant revenue for newspaper companies, but eBay, Craigslist, or banner ads are attracting more and more of that business. In an effort to slash budgets and reduce costs, some newspaper companies have cut their staff. In some cases, newspapers forgo articles from paid

*Future leaders will have to learn to quickly validate information and fuse everything together to make sense of it all.*

professional journalists and use freely submitted entries from the general population. However, the risk of this approach is clear. The end product can be amateurish or inaccurate, or both.

Leaders in the future might suffer similar problems with unscreened incoming information. With ever-increasing access to information, the challenge for leaders and teleworkers alike will be to sift through the flood to validate what is accurate, applicable, and valuable. The leader will have to be a gatekeeper of value, a human filter, to separate the useful from the useless. More important, the leader will have to be a synthesizer of information. With the massive volume of input from various sources, whether they confront internal data captured by the organization's systems, work produced by individual employees, or results of multiple collaborative efforts, leaders will be responsible for blending all the disparate pieces into a meaningful whole.

## The Leader as Converter

It is almost impossible to predict the technologies of tomorrow. The prevalent technologies of Web 3.0, 4.0, or 10.0 can hardly be imagined now. However, future leaders will need to be adaptable and creative to see the value in new technologies and how they can be applied effectively in their organization. Many of the current Web 2.0 technologies, such as blogs and wikis, were not originally intended for business purposes. Who would've thought that technology that was originally popular in creating online dating forums would evolve into trendy social networking sites, and then into business applications for collaboration? YouTube was founded in 2005 as an online video-sharing community, but it didn't take long for businesses to see the value of the site's functionality for creating marketing material. It is up to the leader to make this connection and convert new ideas and new technology to something that will add value to the organization.

We don't want to underestimate the challenge of converting new ideas or technology into tangible solutions and opportunities. It takes some imagination and willingness to take some risks. For example, many organizations are spending time and money in the virtual world Second Life. Second Life allows users to interact through avatars, computer-generated self-images, in a user-defined three-dimensional world. (Think of an advanced social networking site in a virtual 3D reality.)

*Future leaders see the value in new technologies and convert their ideas into tangible results.*

What began as an experiment to allow users to interact and play is now taken seriously by large corporations. Dell can sell PCs through Second Life, Disney promotes movies, Cisco demonstrates new products, and the American Cancer Society has a virtual presence to conduct fundraising. It is unclear if any of these efforts are currently worth the investment, but it is evident that many leaders are already experimenting to convert

Second Life into a viable business opportunity. Perhaps geographically dispersed teleworkers in the future will use the 3D environment to collaborate or simply replace the hallway conversations many traditional workers are accustomed to. While many balk at the idea, leaders in the future will have to craft their own vision and use some imagination to make the ever-changing technologies of tomorrow meet their needs.

## GUIDING PRINCIPLES

The changing organizational and technological landscape is likely to mean that leaders will have to develop a new skill set compared to traditional models. Given the trends in demographics, globalization, and technology, the following skills may become increasingly important for all leaders:

*Balance.* With the shifting demographics of the workforce and increased desires for work–life flexibility, leaders will need to be cognizant of the tension between worker expectations and reality. Workers may want more balance in life, whether it is flexible work arrangements or geographic living conditions. Leaders will have to weigh the desires or needs of their employees against the needs of the organization while keeping employees satisfied in order to continually increase productivity.

*Self-development.* Competing against global talent will be extremely difficult for teleworkers and leaders unless they relentlessly try to acquire new skills, experiences, or knowledge. Staying ahead of the pack will be more difficult than in today's environment. Leaders and employees will require continual training and development.

*Team building.* Teams of tomorrow could experience high turnover rates, which will require leaders to quickly build teams, establish trust, and create solid working relationships virtually in order to consistently deliver results.

# GUIDING PRINCIPLES cont.

*Global thinking.* Teams will become more culturally diverse as teleworking allows more individuals from around the world to participate. Leaders will have to be able to understand the backgrounds or cultures of the people that make up their teams and be sensitive to their different needs, desires, and motivations.

*Collaboration and empowerment.* These two themes go hand in hand since Web 2.0 technologies will make it easier for employees to collaborate and participate outside traditional boundaries. Encouraging collaboration will help the organization develop new ideas or solve problems while the employee is able to be more productive by drawing upon the collective knowledge of anyone who participates. Leaders must learn to promote this behavior by developing relationships founded in trust and commitment and providing workers a degree of autonomy.

*Synthesizing.* With the potential overload of information available, future leaders will need to filter and determine what is accurate, applicable, or valuable. Like fitting pieces of a puzzle together, the task will be to use the various inputs to create a complete picture.

*Imagination and willingness to experiment.* Technologies will continue to evolve and change. Future leaders will have to see the potential value of new technology and how it can be used to add value to the organization.

# AFTERWORD

Throughout this book, we have presented the benefits and challenges of teleworking and recommended that leaders should *want* to lead telework. However, we feel that leaders need to change to keep their organizations competitive or to keep pace with the changing workplace. Technology, globalization, employee expectations, higher costs of traditional working arrangements, and other external factors are converging to make telework a necessity in the near future. Today, organizations are for the most part selective in rolling out telework. Organizations experiment with new work arrangements or offer them to employees as an additional benefit. In the future, we believe telework will become part of normal business operations. Employees will view telework as part of the job, and leaders will be expected to manage teleworkers. In short, today it is an option; tomorrow it will be a requirement.

*Today telework is an option; tomorrow it will be a requirement.*

We also recommend that organizations rethink the entire notion of competitive advantage. For many organizational leaders, competitive advantage comes in the form of financial capital, fixed assets (production plants), or, more commonly, technology. None of this leads to a true competitive advantage—value-creating capacity that cannot be duplicated by others. What leads to a true competitive advantage is the leader. Therefore, we suggest investing in leadership first and technology second. Technology is a tool of the effective manager and leader. Leadership is the game-changer that makes investments in technology worthwhile.

Although there are many similarities in leading traditional workers and teleworkers, much of conventional leadership thinking may become obsolete. Leadership thinking and techniques grounded in physical interaction will become out of place in the virtual world of the future. Leaders who have relied on tactics such as "management by walking around" and building relationships through daily face to face interaction will struggle in the future workplace. New thinking will be required. New tactics will have to be deployed. But leaders have the opportunity now to learn the skills needed in the telework environment.

Organizations will need to take a different approach to developing leaders of the future. Traditional leadership programs may produce competent leaders for today's environment without being adequate for the virtual world. Training and development of the next generation of leaders will have to account for the lack of physical proximity, the expanded access to information, and the increasing need for flexibility. Technological advances will change the workplace at ever-increasing rates, and leaders will need to recognize opportunities and use new tools to accomplish organizational goals. Before organizational leaders invest in leadership training, they need to ask themselves if every dollar spent is going to the leader of the past, present, or future. We hope it is for the latter.

Additionally, leaders need to set the course for their organization and determine the amount of change necessary to compete in the future landscape. Adopting telework may require continuous or transformational changes in the organization. In other words, can telework be woven into the existing fabric of the organization? Or will leaders have to push workers out of their comfort zone, change the organizational culture, and dramatically alter the status quo? Changing behavior and attitudes is not an easy task, but it is often necessary. As quality guru W. Edwards Deming once warned, "Survival is not mandatory." Leaders who wish not only to survive but to succeed in tomorrow's environment will be responsible for driving the evolutionary change in their organizations toward telework.

The ideas in this book may be cutting-edge today, but they will become mainstream tomorrow. The first organizations and countries to recognize this will garner the advantage. Leaders can set themselves apart by exploring telework opportunities now. Even traditional work settings present numerous opportunities to apply technology in more meaningful ways. Rethink personal interactions and how technology can be used to cut through obstacles and across boundaries. Learn to use new tools to collaborate better and become more productive. Welcome the idea of connecting virtually with a broader audience to harness the collective knowledge of all. Realize the benefits of focusing on work rather than on getting to work. Leaders who are not trapped in the present and can keep an eye to the future will reap the benefits of making telework work.

# NOTES

## Introduction

1. Bill Fenson and Sharon Hill, *Implementing and Managing Telework: A Guide for Those Who Make It Happen* (New York: Praeger, 2003).

2. Adrienne Lewis, "As Commutes Begin Earlier, New Daily Routines Emerge," *USA Today,* September 12, 2007, 5A.

3. Stephen Buckner and Joanna Gonzalez, "Americans Spend More Than 100 Hours Commuting to Work Each Year, Census Bureau Reports," U.S. Census Bureau News, March 30, 2005. Available online: www.census.gov/Press-Release/www/releases/archives/american_community_survey_acs/004489.html. Access date: July 23, 2008.

4. "Building Design Leaders Collaborating on Carbon-Neutral Buildings by 2030," U.S. Green Building Council, May 7, 2007. Available online: www.usgbc.org/News/PressReleaseDetails.aspx?ID=3124. Access date: July 23, 2008.

5. "New Poll Reveals 73 Percent of U.S. Workers Want Employers to Be Environmentally Responsible but Lag in Their Own Efforts to Help," Sun Microsystems, August 1, 2007. Available online: www.sun.com/aboutsun/pr/2007-08/sunflash.20070801.1.xml?cid=920966. Access date: July 23, 2008.

6. "Sun's Flexible Business Benefits," *Human Resources* magazine, November 10, 2007. Available online: www.humanresourcesmagazine.com.au /articles/A8/0C051DA8.asp?Type=60&Category=1223. Access date: July 23, 2008.

7. Louise Story, "An Oracle of Oil Predicts $200-a-Barrel Crude," *New York Times,* May 21, 2008.

8. S. A. Snell, C. C. Snow, S. C. Davison, and D. C. Hambrick, "Designing and Supporting Transnational Teams: The Human Resource Agenda," *Human Resource Management Journal* 37, no. 2 (1998): 147–158. Also see

M. Boudreau, K. D. Loch, D. Robey, and D. Straub, "Going Global: Using Information Technology to Advance the Competitiveness of the Virtual Transnational Organization," *Academy of Management Executive* 12, no. 4 (1998): 120–128.

9. Dan Kothsimer, "The Virginia Tech Shootings: A Laboratory Works Together to Overcome Challenges," *Medical Technology Today: ASCP's Newsmagazine for Laboratory Professionals* 4, no. 7 (2007): 390–391.

10. J. Kronholz and S. Fatsis, "Obstacle Course: After Hurricane, Tulane University Struggles to Survive; School Plays Hardball to Keep Students and Tuition Fees; Sabbaticals Get Postponed; 'Looters' Go After Professors," *Wall Street Journal,* September 28, 2005, A1.

## Chapter 1

1. Mark Cotteleer, Edward Inderrieden, and Felissa Lee, "Selling the Sales Force on Automation," *Harvard Business Review* 84, nos. 7/8 (2006): 18–22.

## Chapter 5

1. Bill Munck, "Changing a Culture of Face Time," *Harvard Business Review* 79, no. 10 (November 2001): 125–128, 130–131.

## Chapter 6

1. Al Sacco, "Expensive and Dangerous," *CIO,* November 15, 2007, 14.

## Chapter 7

1. Kira Vermond, "Death of the 9 to 5 Workday," *Globe and Mail,* December 7, 2007. Available online: www.reportonbusiness.com/servlet/story/RTGAM.20071207.wkiravermond1207/BNStory/robAtWork/home. Access date: July 27, 2008.

2. Rita Zeidner, "Absence Makes the Team Uneasy: Survey Undermines Traditional Thinking About Teleworking," Society for Human Resource Management, *HR Technology Hot Topics,* March 2008.

3. Barbara Presley Noble, "Earning It: Nudging Workers from Company Nests," The New York Times, July 30, 1995. http://query.nytimes.com/gst/fullpage.htm/?res=990ce3dd103cf933a05754c0963958260&sec=&spon=&&scp=2&sq=Earning%20It%20It%20Nudging&st=cse. Accessed 3/13/09.

4. Stephanie Overby, "Intel's E-mail Overload Solution," *CIO*, June 22, 2007. Available online: www.cio.com/article/120852/Intel_rsquo_s_E_ Mail_ Overload_Solution. Access date: July 27, 2008.

5. Thomas Wailgum, "Information Overload Is Killing You and Your Productivity," CIO, January 4, 2008. Available online: www.cio.com/article/169200. Access date: July 27, 2008.

6. Ibid.

7. Vanessa Ho, "Remote Workers Indulge in Risky Behavior," Integrated mar.com Corporation, February 24, 2008. Available online: www.echannelline.com/usa/story.cfm?item=22969. Access date: July 27, 2008.

## *Chapter 8*

1. Jonathan Lore, "Five Lessons from a U.S.–English Merger," *Quality Progress* 37, no. 11 (2004): 30.

2. Don Tapscott and Anthony D. Williams, *Wikinomics: How Mass Collaboration Changes Everything* (New York: Penguin, 2006).

3. L. Gordon Crovitz, "From Wikinomics to Government 2.0," *Wall Street Journal Online*, May 12, 2008. Available online: http://online.wsj.com/article/SB121055303906183983.html?mod=todays_columnists. Access date: August 4, 2008.

# ABOUT THE AUTHORS

A former military intelligence officer, **Evan Offstein** is a graduate of the U.S. Military Academy at West Point. After earning a doctorate in business from Virginia Tech, he joined the business management faculty at Frostburg State University. Offstein is the author of *Stand Your Ground: Building Honorable Leaders the West Point Way* (Praeger, 2006). Based on the success of this book and his honorable leadership research, he has enjoyed national acclaim and has landed numerous speaking engagements and consulting contracts for such organizations as the U.S. Army, Northwestern Mutual Life, Allegany College, Southwest Florida Law Enforcement Academy, Raymond James Financial, Securian's Tax and Financial Group, Wheeling Jesuit University, Solutia Corporation, Virginia Association of Volunteer Rescue Squads, GreenApple Schools, Indiana University of Pennsylvania, Idaho Law Enforcement Academy, Human Resource Development Commission, Century Furniture, CHEP International, Maryland Transportation Authority, and the Western Maryland Health System. Recently, he was awarded Frostburg State's Faculty Achievement Award for Excellence in Scholarship and Research.

**Jason M. Morwick** is a graduate of the U.S. Military Academy at West Point and a former army officer. He earned an MBA degree from Regis University, Denver, Colorado. Currently a full-time teleworker Morwick has managed teams and organizations at General Electric, Cisco Systems, and CHEP USA, a Brambles Company. He has worked in a variety of positions, including operations manager and director of human resources. Morwick has trained hundreds of employees in Six Sigma, diversity, project management, communication, and leadership. Moreover, he has published in esteemed journals such as *Quality*

*Progress, Review of Business,* and *Business Journal.* Additionally, he is a speaker and consultant on leadership, communication, and business process improvement. Feel free to contact either Evan or Jason at www.teleworkleaders.com.

# INDEX